Letters from Stalag Luft 3

Letters from Stalag Luft 3

A TALE OF TWO HEROES

One fought the Nazis - the other, an invisible enemy.
This is their story.

For George from John.

John Garwell

First paperback edition
Book design by Publishing Push

Paperback: 978-1-80227-758-6
eBook: 978-1-80227-759-3

For Hannah, Tom, Amelia and Lauren.

Contents

Prologue

December 2012 – the day before my mother died. We are sitting in her neat care home room; the bed is made, and she is dressed. I look at her lined face, her unkempt hair, her sunken eyes, her cheeks hollowed out by ninety-one long years, and the slow, relentless march of dementia. She still knows who I am. She is still my mother.

As far as it is possible, dementia has been kind to her; she gets confused, yes, but the old anxieties have all but gone. She can still laugh, and she can still sing. Right now, I can hear her quietly humming 'The Red Flag' – not because of any political sympathies, not for any reason at all – just the random recall of a half-forgotten melody. Mum doesn't know it's her last day, and neither do I.

There is a newspaper open on her lap – the Daily Express. She slowly turns the pages and looks absently at each one. Nothing registers. And then she stops, suddenly attentive. It's a photograph of a Lancaster bomber from World War II. She says nothing, but her frail hand reaches out, and a finger slowly traces its outline. She can still remember him.

For as long as I can recall, the letters had been bundled together in an old paper carrier bag, half-forgotten under a jumble of family memorabilia: old box camera black and white photographs, studio portraits of babies and grandparents in sepia, faded snaps of '70s weddings with flared trousers and chest-wide lapels, old school reports (*'John has shown interest in his work but is inclined to daydream.'*) and children's crayon pictures – the sort that mums can never throw away.

The letters are from a Nazi prisoner of war camp – the famous one – Stalag Luft 3. Written in faded pencil on delicate airmail paper and stamped by the German censor, they are from a young man in his early twenties, some addressed to his family and some to his sweetheart back home. I am his son. Amongst them, and there are over fifty, is just one from her to him. It's addressed by Miss Joan Shepherd to Flight Lieutenant A.J. Garwell D.F.C. D.F.M. Prisoner of War No 117, Stalag Luft 3, Germany, and dated 15th December 1944. It starts like this:

'My Dearest Love,

I've had some wizard letters from you lately written in late August & September. You don't seem one tiny little bit different from when you first went away & that makes me very happy. The most wonderful thing of all is to read that you continue to love me just as I love you. I often think what a wonderful thing our love is to stand so many tests, and dearest, my only wish is that by loving me and having my love, you have been helped in your long and dreary wait for freedom. You know, Arthur, sometimes my longing for you has almost been torture. I've prayed to God to bring you home to me soon and wept tears into my pillow at night for sheer loneliness for you, and then I've thought of that wonderful day when you come home, and the joy of that will dim the memory of these days of waiting.'

The letter never reached him. Rubber stamped on the reverse are these words:

> *'This letter formed part of unreceived mails which fell into the hands of the allied forces in Germany. It is undeliverable as addressed and is therefore returned to you.'*

Undeliverable because he was already on the long march to liberation and home.

This is the story of two young people caught up in the vortex of war, who they were, how they survived, and what became of their hopes and dreams.

CHAPTER 1

Hexham, Northumberland

'Letter home from POW 117, Stalag Luft 3.

29th June 1944

Dear Family,

I haven't received any mail from you this month, but I trust that you are all fit and well. The shortage is due, I assume, to the cessation of airmail from England. I wonder if you have been receiving my letters satisfactorily. Things are going very well here. The last few days have been perfect. The old garden is growing very well. Should have a good crop of tomatoes this year and probably some onions. Hoping to have some flowers too. How is 'Viewlands' looking? Let me see – it's June – you should have a fine display of roses. How I wish I was sitting on the train somewhere between Corbridge and Hexham and could look up and see the house on the hilltop. I can picture it very clearly now in my mind – though I find it difficult to imagine so much green all around. You know we haven't much green here – only the dirty dark green of pine trees.

Well, I am hoping to be with you fairly soon now – maybe before all the roses have died off! I definitely expect to have Christmas with you anyway.

Cheerio. Lots of love. Arthur.'

The train to Hexham follows the Tyne valley out of Newcastle and heads due west, hugging the southern bank of the wide, slow-moving river. Through Prudhoe, Stocksfield, Riding Mill, and the once Roman garrison town of Corbridge, the valley gradually steepens as rural Northumberland unfolds, and Hexham approaches. To this day, if you know where to look, you can just make out a house high up to the right, exactly where the sky meets the horizon – 'Viewlands' – my father's family home.

Leave the station, cross the bridge over the Tyne's broad expanse, away from the town and its ancient Abbey, and head up the steeply twisting, tree-lined Oakwood Bank beyond. Up and up, skirting Oakwood village, until the last few scattered houses abruptly end, and the narrow lane continues on towards Hadrian's Wall. There it sits, red brick and four-square, looking out across the wide sweep of the Tyne valley to the rolling hills beyond.

He'd lived at 'Viewlands' from the age of eleven. It was 1931 when his mother and father first turned the key to the back door and stepped inside the new home that had just been built for them. Detached, with fields all around, a French door, a bay window, and its own garage, it was more than just a house move; it was a big step up Hexham's social ladder - especially for an ex-coal miner like Arthur's dad, and in the thick of the Great Depression.

Think of pit heads, winding gear, and the grime-lined faces of coal miners, and you probably won't picture this part of Northumberland. It's famed for picture-postcard views of the wall that marked the northern boundary of the Roman Empire and for the wild, empty country beyond, but not mining. There's little to see of it now, but for hundreds of years, local men worked the coal and lead mines at nearby Acomb. It was a hard life for meagre wages, and it was where his father, also called Arthur, worked as a hewer at the coal face as a young man. There were few other options.

Gentle in nature, with a soft, lilting, Geordie accent, Arthur senior was not an ambitious man, but in 1917, as the 1st World War neared its end, and after serving in the Royal Army Medical Corps, his life changed - he got married. Nothing unusual in that, except for the woman he chose; her name was Sarah Pearson, one of five sisters and three brothers from the coastal town of Whitehaven in Cumberland. Straight-backed, no-nonsense, and a natural organiser, she would shape his future.

By February 1920, they had their first child and christened him Arthur John after his father. Young Arthur inherited his grandmother's red hair and his mother's slim build – physical characteristics that would mark him out for the rest of his life. A sister, Beatrice, followed two years later.

Beatrice & Arthur

It might have been the 'Roaring Twenties' for some, but there was little to see of it in rural Northumberland; times were tough, and money was tight. Nothing remotely useful would be thrown away. A pair of worn socks would be darned time and again until there was more darning than socks. Only then would they be taken to a woman in Acomb village who made a few pennies by knitting a new foot-bed onto the uppers. The very few might afford the luxury of a motor car; everyone else walked, rode a bicycle, or took the bus. In this exposed and hilly county, cycling involved a lot of walking.

When Sarah had relatives to visit in Aspatria, Cumberland, sixty miles to the west, she got there on her heavy 'sit-up-and-beg' bicycle - sixty miles of up and down into the prevailing westerly wind. *"T'winds in your face!"* she heard shouted from the roadside. At least the same wind would hopefully blow her the sixty miles home.

She was enterprising, hard-working, and quick-thinking. While taking her toddler son into town on the bus in his best sailor suit, he was suddenly, violently sick. In an instant, she whipped off his hat to catch it. No fuss, no drama – that was her way.

When her husband got the chance to move on from the dirty, dangerous life of a coal miner, it was her that made it happen. He had a workmate and best friend who'd got out already and gone to be an agent for Pearl Assurance in Hexham. *"Why don't you try it, Arthur?"* he'd been asked but did nothing about it. Not, that is, until his wife got behind him. And so, it came to be that he swapped a tin hat for a trilby and a blue collar for white.

In those days, an insurance agent went from door to door to collect premiums, deal with claims and find new customers. He was a natural at it – friendly, sociable, conscientious, and well-liked in the local community. He might cycle on his rounds, but he wore a suit and a crisp white shirt. Things were looking up, but it would be many years before the move to 'Viewlands.'

The land had been bought first – just a small corner of a farmer's field up the hill from Oakwood village – but there was no money to build a house. That would have to wait. It called for thrift and patience.

As the 1920s gave way to the new decade, the family home they had hoped for finally became a possibility. Plans were drawn up and finances arranged. By the time the house was built, their third child was on its way, a daughter, christened Nora.

In 1933, as Adolph Hitler became the Chancellor of Germany, life in Hexham went on much as usual. Church and community were at the centre of family life; Arthur senior, who possessed a fine voice, sang in the Abbey choir, and the children attended Sunday school. There were harvest festivals, church fetes, and market days in Hexham's ancient town centre – a picture of English tradition.

The south-facing garden at 'Viewlands' was soon planted with fruit trees, vegetables, and flowers – especially roses.

'Letter home 27th Sept 1944

> *How did the garden go this year? Is the soil still as heavy as it used to be, or has it broken down much in the last three years? And do you still have those marvellous displays of rambling roses? But I mustn't talk about it too much, or I will make myself homesick!'*

Milk was collected daily from the farm just down the lane, and drinking water was drawn up from below ground with an old-fashioned hand pump in the kitchen. The pantry was stocked with local produce, and meals were cooked with a mother's diligent care. Coal fires kept the house warm when winter brought its bitter easterly winds and deep snow. A row of tobacco-stained pipes sat in a rack by Arthur senior's favourite armchair next to the living room fireplace. The children flourished in settled family life.

Young Arthur was a bright boy and passed the exams that would earn him a place at Hexham's Queen Elizabeth Grammar School. There were fees to pay, though, and that would stretch the family budget, but the money was found. It wasn't wasted. He worked hard and did well while the world outside grew darker.

Then came another step up the social ladder – the purchase of a motor car – a second-hand Ford.

*'Letter home Aug 7*th*, 1942*

> *What's happening to the old car these days? You never seem to mention it. You haven't hit another cow, have you? Go easy on those chickens you speak of. I shall expect about twelve to a meal when I get back on the right side again.'*

Early in 1939, with Arthur's grammar school education completed, it was time to think about finding a career. He sat the entrance examination for His Majesty's Customs and Excise, passed, and was appointed to join the local branch in Hexham. In May of the same year, he joined the RAF Volunteer Reserve.

The RAF Volunteer Reserve had been formed in 1936 as the threat of war loomed and the need to recruit trained pilots grew ever more urgent. Up until then, RAF pilots were selected from the ranks of the socially advantaged and, once commissioned, joined a jealously guarded elite. But that would no longer be enough – the net needed to be cast much wider. The new Volunteer Reserve opened up access to young men who would otherwise have no chance of flying. Lads from all social backgrounds could apply and be accepted for training if they were bright enough. The aim was to make it as easy as possible for reservists to learn to fly while living at home and holding down a civilian job. Flying training would take place on alternate weekends at aerodrome centres that had been set up around the country. The target was to provide 60 hours of flying time in a year. Weekday evenings would be used for ground instruction. When training was completed, men were enrolled as sergeants rather than officers, with commissions available later for all who proved their worth. By the outbreak of war in September 1939, the scheme had produced over 6,000 RAF pilots in just three and a half years. Young Arthur, barely out of his teens, was to be one of them.

With initial training completed and having gained his pilot 'Wings,' he was posted to an RAF Operational Training Unit. The O.T.U's provided a three-month course that specialised in one kind of flying, either fighter or bomber, night-time or daylight operations. There were 152 of them at home and abroad. His was to be No. 14 O.T.U. based at RAF Cottesmore in the county of Rutland. Formed in April 1940, its purpose was to train night bomber crews.

So that was it. He was going to be a 'Bomber Boy.'

The Garwell family - Sarah, Arthur, Nora, Beatrice
& Arthur Jnr. Summer 1932.

CHAPTER 2

Doncaster, Yorkshire

My father's formative years were spent in a stable, loving family and in a close, rural community – a solid foundation from which to face the chaotic times that lay ahead. My mother's early years were very different. Her letter – the one that never reached Stalag Luft 3 – includes this short paragraph:

> 'It's a week now since I came to stay at 'Viewlands' for the duration, and I can't tell you how much happier and content I've been in this gay little house on the hill. Family life is a wonderful thing, and it's the first real taste I've had of it since I was nine years old, and Christmas is almost here too.'

She was born in Northampton on 14th August 1920. The birth certificate names her father as Albert Shepherd – a motor mechanic – and her mother as Edith Mary Shepherd, formally Scammell. Joan was their firstborn child. Three years later, a baby brother arrived. He was named Peter.

Joan and Peter.

The family moved north for work - to the West Riding of Yorkshire; Albert had obtained employment as a mechanic and chauffeur for a wealthy farmer - a job that came with a tied cottage at a place called Rose Hill, close by to Doncaster Racecourse, famous for the St Leger - the world's oldest classic horse race.

Doncaster was an industrial town; there were coal mines, steel mills, railway yards, locomotive works, tractor manufacturers, and even confectioners (Butterscotch was invented there along with Nuttall's Mintoes and Murray Mints - the 'too good to hurry mints'). It was a largely working-class community.

"Daddy was a snob," my mother often said. *"He wouldn't let us speak with a Yorkshire accent."* That was a tough rule to inflict on kids newly moved in from the south and attending their local school for the first time. They suffered name calling and bullying – especially little Peter, who was easily intimidated. His big sister, herself a sensitive child, took on the role of his protector.

Albert Shepherd didn't see himself as a snob, but he had ambitions coupled with a natural flair for engineering. He took himself off to night school to gain qualifications and became, eventually, an Associate Member of the Institute of Mechanical Engineers (AMIMechE).

The family settled into life at Rose Hill. The children loved sneaking off to the racecourse to lay under the hedge at the track's edge and feel the ground shake as a hundred hooves thundered past. They were bright kids, and life seemed pretty normal. Then a surprise; their mum was expecting, and in 1927, a baby sister arrived. She was christened June. Everyone loved little June, especially her big sister, Joan: *"As soon as I came home from school, I just wanted to pick her up and put her on my lap. I can still remember what her tiny hands were like."*

It was coming up to Christmas in 1929 when little June fell ill with TB meningitis, an aggressive bacterial infection that starts in the lungs and then attacks the tissues covering the brain. Although Alexander Fleming had already discovered penicillin, antibiotics would not come into common use until the 1940s. In those days, there was no other treatment; doctors could do little more than hold a child's hand and hope. Back then, on average, one in every twenty infants died of untreatable infectious diseases. June was one of them. She was just two years old.

It was a devastating blow. A pall of grief hung over the house in Rose Hill, but worse was to come. As spring approached, Edith, who had nursed her infant child with all the tender care a mother can muster, herself fell prey to the same contagious illness. By Whitsun, she too had succumbed.

For nine-year-old Joan and six-year-old Peter, nothing would ever be the same again. Their father had to work long hours and somehow provide care for his children; all he could do was take on a housekeeper. The first one stole jewellery from the household and was dismissed. More turmoil, and then Albert lost his job and the tied cottage that went with it.

There followed, over the next eight years, a succession of different places to live. For a while, Albert took a rented house, but that required a housekeeper and was too expensive, so for the most part, rooms were rented - "digs," as my mother called them. A landlady could keep an eye on the children when Albert was at work - at least that was the idea. Some cared, some didn't. Some scolded, and at least one, Miss Piper, was a touch eccentric - if donning a tea cosy to keep your head warm and save a little fuel in the winter counts as eccentricity.

Eventually, Albert met someone else and married for a second time; her name was Emmie Stanniland. Emmie's relationship with the children was cool, to say the least. *"I was sent away to Northampton to train to be a nurse,"* Mum often said, with the emphasis on *"sent."* She was just seventeen.

Soon after arriving, it all went wrong. While training to apply wound dressings, she was asked to replace the bandages of a child with a badly burned arm. She started to unwind the dressing from the top, but as the livid flesh came into view, her nerve failed. She ran out of the ward in tears. These days it would be recognised as a panic attack, and maybe some allowance made, but not back then. She was sent home in disgrace, her nursing career over. Her father was more angry than understanding, and she did not receive a warm welcome. The relationship was breaking down.

For a short while, she got a job as a nanny looking after the two young children of a doctor and his wife, both of whom held unfashionably liberal views on how to raise their offspring. Discipline of any sort was forbidden, regardless of behaviour. It was not going to be easy. This is a story I clearly remember my mother telling me as a child; how their ever more challenging tantrums finally came to a head over the breakfast table. It involved a plate of cereal and a petulant refusal to cooperate with Nanny's gentle encouragement to eat at least some of it. It ended when a plate of soggy cornflakes flew across the room and landed, with unerring accuracy, in Nanny's lap. This earned the offending child a bit of a scolding and a reproachful tap on the arm by way of emphasis. A natural enough reaction, perhaps, but not one that met with the approval of two doting parents when the child in question ran to them for comfort. Nanny was fired on the spot.

That made two successive career failures in a row and even more disapproval from Albert Shepherd.

Relief came from an unexpected quarter; Emmie's mother, Mrs Stanniland, offered to give Joan a home at her little terraced house in Flowitt Street, Hexthorpe. Known to all as Blossom, Mrs Stanniland took young Joan under her wing like a mother hen. It was just what she needed.

But what about her brother, Peter? As the fateful year of 1939 arrived, Albert gave written consent for his son to enter a three-year apprenticeship with the RAF to train as an aero engine fitter. In January, Peter left home for good. He was fifteen years old - still a child.

War broke out in September. Joan was nineteen. She had grown into an attractive young woman with an hourglass figure, a prowess for sport, especially tennis, and a love of fashion and music. It was the time of swing bands like Glenn Miller and of wild dance styles like the jitterbug - antidotes to the fear and uncertainty that hung heavily in the air. With her best pal, Norrie Butterfield, she took to the dance floors of Doncaster with youthful exuberance.

To meet her then would give little clue to the vulnerability that hid just below the surface. Scars inflicted in childhood last a lifetime.

Joan & her best pal, Norrie Butterfield.

CHAPTER 3

Operational Training

By May 1940, nine months after war was declared, Arthur had learned how to fly. Now he had to learn how to go to war. In three months. Aged twenty.

These were desperate times for the country: German armies had swept through the Netherlands, Belgium, and France, and what remained of the British Expeditionary Force was pinned with its back to the sea on the beaches of Dunkirk. Faced with surrender or annihilation, an audacious plan to evacuate as many troops as possible was hatched; it was codenamed Operation Dynamo. Over 800 civilian boats of all shapes and sizes crossed the English Channel to rescue the troops, many of whom had been waiting for hours chest-deep in seawater. Between 26th May and 4th June, some 330,000 men were plucked to safety. It was a barely credible but deeply humbling retreat.

Some politicians, now fearing the imminent conquest of the British Isles by Nazi forces, wanted to sue for a peace deal with Hitler. Prime Minister Churchill did not:

"We shall go on to the end. We shall fight in France, we shall fight on the seas and oceans, we shall fight with growing confidence and growing strength in the air, we shall defend our island, whatever

the cost may be. We shall fight on the beaches, we shall fight on the landing grounds, we shall fight in the fields and in the streets, we shall fight in the hills; we shall never surrender."

Fighting with *'growing confidence and growing strength in the air'* required trained airmen, and there were nowhere near enough. At this precise moment, at the beginning of June, Arthur started his final three months of intensive training.

Arriving at RAF Cottesmore, surrounded by the patchwork fields and sleepy villages of the county of Rutland, Flight Sergeant Garwell was one of a large new intake of men assigned to the next training course. Young men from home and abroad, from as far away as New Zealand, Australia, and Rhodesia - all newly trained in different aircrew trades - were gathered together in a large mess hall and left to mingle, the idea being to let new crews select themselves informally. For the Hampden bomber aircraft in use at No.14 O.T.U., each crew required four men: a pilot, a navigator, a wireless operator, and a gunner. Two might pair up having known each other from earlier training; they would then cast round for the other skills required - like a rock band looking for a drummer and a bass player. Crews forged this way stayed together, building the mutual trust needed to look death in the face night after night.

Medium height, thin as a rake, and with a mop of wavy red hair, 'Ginger' Garwell (as he got to be called) took to the role of crew leadership naturally. With his father's affable nature and his mother's steely core, he could foster friendship and inspire confidence in equal measure. Both would be needed soon enough.

And so, to his place of work.

Imagine learning to drive in a small car, only to be handed the keys to a 44-tonne articulated truck. Compared with learning to fly in a tiny Tiger Moth biplane, a Handley Page Hampden medium range twin engine bomber seemed like a giant. It was a workhorse of Bomber Command and a weapon of choice for Operational Training Unit 14. Maybe not choice - the O.T.U's got what they were given - mainly tired cast-offs that operational squadrons had finished with. Malfunctions were common.

Big on the outside, tiny inside; at just three feet wide, the pilot's cockpit was so cramped that the Hampden was nicknamed the 'flying suitcase' by its crews. Fast and maneuverable with a long, slender tail section like a dragonfly. It was beautiful to fly but terrible to fly in. There were no dual controls and no room for an instructor to sit next to the pilot. Two weeks of ground instruction and a flight instruction card with how to take off on one side and how to land on the other, followed by a few flights with an instructor on board, and that was about it. Young Arthur had to learn how to operate 111 separate controls off by heart.

Each of the four crew members sat alone in a different section of the aircraft, visually isolated. The pilot got in by climbing up a ladder to a narrow walkway on the port wing and then clambering into his seat through a sliding hatch in the cockpit canopy. The rest of the crew entered through a door by the rear under-gunner's compartment. For the navigator, getting to the front involved scrambling up through the narrow fuselage, past oxygen bottles, hydraulic pipes, fire extinguishers, and cables, then struggling over the massive spar that held the wings together to arrive behind the pilot. Then it was feet first through a crawlspace beneath the pilot's seat to finally arrive in a Perspex bubble which was the nose cockpit - not easy in a bulky flying suit with a parachute pack.

It was virtually impossible for other crew members to move an injured pilot in mid-flight. Training for this eventuality had to be scrubbed after several fatal crashes - and crashes were frequent enough without avoidable ones. Training was a dangerous business.

The Hampden's defensive guns (one up front, plus an upper and lower gunner behind) were no match for enemy fighter planes in daylight raids: for one thing, the gun turrets couldn't swivel to fire sideways, a shortcoming easily exploited by attackers. So, very early on, it was decided to only operate under cover of darkness. That would involve long sorties to targets as far away as Berlin - a round trip of almost nine and a half hours in an aircraft that would run out of fuel and fall out of the sky after ten. Many Hampdens were lost this way.

Travelling in a modern commercial airliner today gives not the remotest idea of the physical demands and risks involved in flying a WW2 bomber at medium to high altitudes. Air temperatures as low as -40c in a non-pressurised, barely heated cabin called for many layers of the thickest protective clothing. There were no toilets and no room to move if there had been. Any crew member 'caught short' on a long flight had no choice but to relieve himself where he sat. A flying suit in sub-zero temperatures, threaded with unreliable electric heating filaments, was hazardous enough without being wet through from the inside. Internally fitted rubber tubing was thought to be a solution, but the liquid discharged could fuse a flying boot to the floor in a solid block of ice.

High altitude flights required oxygen masks which, along with aircraft instruments and controls, could ice up and fail in the lowest temperatures. Without sufficient oxygen, crews risked a condition called anoxia with its symptoms of confusion, numbness, dizziness, and vomiting, followed by lack of consciousness. Four minutes without oxygen and the brain begins to die. It could, and did, prove fatal.

Navigation, especially early on in the war, was rudimentary. It involved maps and compasses and visual identification of landmarks in the darkness below, often by moonlight. Low clouds and foul weather were frequent enemies. It was very easy to get lost. Morse code was the only contact with base - a brief message when and if a target was hit, and another within thirty miles of the English coast before landing. Bomber crews were on their own. Many returned to find the low-lying expanses of eastern England shrouded in fog, with fuel running out and little time to find an alternative landing place. Some ditched in the sea, others crashed.

When it came to survival, no crew member was more or less important than another; each skill was vital. A few young men, faced with the reality of approaching warfare, were crippled by anxiety. The RAF had a label for this - LMF, short for 'lack of moral fibre' and those suffering from it were quietly shuffled away to a non-combat role, the attendant stigma hanging as heavily around their necks as a dead albatross. No trainee wanted that to happen, so, for the most part, fears were suppressed, not shared. Camaraderie and the bravado of youth prevailed.

Just one month into this intense training course, in July 1940, and with France newly defeated, Nazi Germany turned the full might of its air force – the Luftwaffe – against Britain. Hitler's aim was simple – to totally destroy the RAF and force the country into a negotiated settlement, or complete capitulation. The infamous 'Battle of Britain' had begun. As wave after wave of Messerschmitt fighters ripped into the Hurricanes and Spitfires of the RAF in the blue skies above Southern England, the motivation to complete training and engage with a rampant enemy could not have been higher.

Forty miles south of Cottesmore, in the tiny Bedfordshire village of Melchbourne, St Mary Magdalene Church nestles quietly among graceful trees. Inside, on a small plinth, stands a single, twisted propeller blade – a poignant memorial to the crew of Hampden P1305, which crashed on Friday 19th August 1940. They were from O.T.U. 14 and from the same intake of trainees as my father. This is a brief account of what happened to them:

> *'Took off from RAF Cottesmore on a navigation exercise. The aircraft was observed to emerge from the cloud base, diving almost vertically, and crashed and exploded near the Dower House at Melchbourne, Bedfordshire, scattering wreckage over a wide area. Some sources suggest that the pilot lost control while practicing use of oxygen and changing seats.'*

The four young men who lost their lives on that summer's day were:

Pilot Officer William King from Nottingham, age 20.
Sergeant Stanley Britnor from Ashton Under Lyne, Lancashire, age 26.
Sergeant John Bishop from Cheadle, Staffordshire, age 20.
Sergeant John Jackson from Sunderland, Co. Durham, age 19.

They were just four of some 8,000 volunteer airmen who lost their lives in accidents while training or on non-operational duties during the war.

Days later, at the end of August, my father, his crew, and all the other trainees lucky enough to survive the course left Cottesmore to join their operational squadrons.

CHAPTER 4

Into Battle

January 2019. A blanket of slate grey cloud clings to the hilltops of the Aire valley. I push my bike through the front door and out into the slanting, icy rain. It's what I did back then on a Saturday morning - no excuses. Nine miles down the road, in Keighley, a small group of like-minded cyclists are huddled, waiting for the ride to start. It's the Aire Valley Solutions lads, known, tongue-in-cheek, as the '9 am Old Boys.' I am the oldest boy on this particular morning - by some margin.

As we reach the market town of Skipton, my younger brother, Tim, hooks on to the back of the group. The pace is brisk and cold legs begin to warm up. Through Carleton, Broughton, and Gargrave, the speed gradually increases as the short, sharp climbs and the nagging headwind take their toll. I decide it's time to slide to the back and let them go. My brother stays with me, bless him.

We arrive at the cafe in Airton, within sight of Malham Cove's misty limestone crag, and lean our bikes against the wall outside a little later than the rest. Water drips from our gloves. Inside, a large cafetiere of rich Italian coffee and two toasted teacakes soon arrive to start the gradual recovery process.

Tim takes a small plastic bag from his back pocket and places it on the table in front of me. *"I've brought you this,"* he says. Unfolding it curiously, I take out a silver-coloured, engine-turned cigarette case. Something inside it rattles. Pressing the catch, I prise it carefully open, and out fall two small metal tags. One is octagonal and stamped A.J. Garwell. OFFR. C.E. 65503 – his RAF identity tag. The other, threaded at one end with a piece of rough string, is stamped Stalag Luft 3 and the number 117 – his prisoner of war identity tag. I'd never seen them before.

"Look at this," Tim says, pointing to the gold-coloured interior of the cigarette case. Scratched by hand in a neat column are the names of seventeen European cities: Berlin, Magdeburg, Kiel, Hamburg, Wilhelmshaven, Bremen, Emden, Cologne, Gelsenkirchen, Bordeaux, Essen, L'Orient, Vannes, Brest, Le Havre, Amsterdam and Duisberg. To the right of the column is scratched 'Total 30' – the number of raids in his first tour of duty.

———

It is said that the chance of surviving those first thirty raids was one in three at best. The riskiest operations were the first five, when mistakes by novice crews were most likely, and the last five, when luck was fast running out.

———

In September 1940, Pilot Sergeant Garwell and his newly trained crew were posted to 83 Squadron based at RAF Scampton, six miles north of the Cathedral City of Lincoln, in the heart of 'Bomber County.' By that time, the whole of Continental Europe had been defeated by the Nazi onslaught; only the British Isles remained defiant. The Luftwaffe's attempt to cripple the RAF in preparation for an all-out amphibious invasion had failed, so Hitler's strategy changed: on Saturday the 7th of September, London was attacked in a mass German bombing raid. It was the start of the 'Blitz.' London was bombed nightly for the next 57 days. Raids spread out to cities across the land, hitting civilian populations, industrial centres, and ports. Over 40,000 British citizens died before it ended.

At the start of the war Franklin D. Roosevelt, President of the neutral United States, issued an appeal to the opposing forces to confine their air raids to military targets and avoid bombing civilian populations. The British agreed in principle, as long as their enemies reciprocated. It didn't last.

Despite the bombs raining down on London, Hampden crews at 83 Squadron were still being sent to attack predominantly military targets, especially German naval bases and U-boat pens, one of which was likely the first destination for a rookie crew fresh out of training. But where exactly? As the door to the briefing room pushed open, and four young men entered for the first time, they must have wondered what was in store for them that night. Whether they felt fear, excitement, or both, it was likely hidden beneath a veneer of black humour typical of RAF bomber crews.

Enemy shipping based in French ports like Le Havre or L'Orient was closest - it was easier to get in and out quickly with a better chance of dodging the anti-aircraft flak. German ports like Kiel or Wilhelmshaven were a tougher proposition but still on the coast and easy enough to spot on a clear night. It was the targets deeper into Germany that offered the greatest challenge - heavily defended cities like Duisberg, Essen, or Gelsenkirchen in the industrial heartland of the Ruhr Valley or, worse still, Berlin, the most heavily defended city of all and at the very limit of the Hampden's range.

Wherever the destination of that first operation, there was a lot of vital information to be understood and absorbed at the briefing. The Intelligence Officer revealed the exact target and the defences that might lay in wait. The Signals Officer detailed which home airfield identification beacons to look for on return. The Armoury Officer announced the bomb load and type, and the Engineer gave the fuel load. Then the Met. Officer gave the expected weather, including cloud cover and wind speeds for the outward and return journeys. They would be hoping for a clear moonlit night. Finally, take-off times for each aircraft were given. In the early 1940s, bombers were sent individually to reduce the risk of being spotted and attacked by enemy fighter planes. Garwell's crew would be flying into battle for the first time, completely alone.

After the briefing, it was time to study the charts and maps and plot the exact route, identifying landmarks such as rivers, lakes, or railway junctions that could be easily spotted by moonlight thousands of feet below.

Early on in the war, navigation methods were, to say the least, basic. If cloud cover was encountered, the navigator took the last fixed point and, using a compass, calculated where the aircraft was based on its speed, direction of travel, and the likely effect of the wind. It was called 'dead reckoning' and, although it involved some complex mathematics, was often little better than guesswork – the risk of getting hopelessly lost was almost as great as the risk from enemy action.

Preparations completed, there was nothing to do but rest, have a meal, and hope for the best. Then, at last, dressed in their heavy flying clothing, make their way to the bomber crouching in darkness at the end of the runway. Stomachs tightened. This was it.

Wherever that first raid took them, they got back in one piece - as they did from each successive operation until early November. Other crews from 83 Squadron were not so lucky; on the 28th of September at 4:50 am, Hampden P4381 ran out of fuel returning from L'Orient and smashed into St Matthias church in Lincoln, exploding on impact. The crew had already bailed out, but only three of the four crew members survived. Such incidents were an almost daily occurrence for returning bombers.

Life for the Hampden crews of 83 Squadron was one of total contrasts - short periods of intense danger through long dark nights followed by a cooked breakfast back at base, a sleep, and maybe a potter down to the local pub in the quiet English countryside the next evening. Then came the wait for the next brush with death.

Each sortie that Garwell's crew survived was one more ticked off the thirty. Their luck held out until the night of Sunday, 3rd November. It happened to be the first night that London was peaceful after 57 consecutive days of bombing by the Luftwaffe. Details of what happened are sparse: it was shortly after take-off - Hampden P4392 was heading south over Lincoln with a full bomb load. Clearing the city but still very low, Garwell turned the aircraft steeply to port to pick up the planned flight path east. All the records say is that the Hampden's speed was too low to make the turn. Within seconds they were out of control and heading for the ground at 100 miles an hour. The aircraft hit a tree and smashed into the open countryside near the village of Fiskerton, just five miles East of Lincoln Cathedral. Incredibly, all four crew members crawled from the wreckage unhurt.

The cause? Everything points towards 'stabilized yaw' - a known flaw in the Hampden's design; turn too steeply at too low a speed, and the front of the aircraft blocks the airflow over the tail, causing the rudders to lock and the pilot to lose control. It was a hard way to learn that lesson.

Looking back on it, maybe they thought they'd got their bad luck out of the way. If so, they were wrong.

One week later, on Sunday 10th November, Hampden X2964 taxied to the end of Scampton's runway, turned, and waited for clearance to take off, its bomb bay fully loaded. It was 1:35 am. Aboard were Pilot Sgt Garwell, Sgt Kirke, Sgt Flux, and Sgt White. Cockpit drills completed, the two Bristol Pegasus 9-cylinder, 980 horsepower engines roared to full power as throttles were opened and brakes released. The bomber lurched forward and started to gain speed. As the noise and vibration increased to a crescendo, Pilot Sgt Garwell pulled the control column sharply back to get her airborne, but something was wrong - she was not responding. Now covering the ground at eighty-five miles an hour, the end of the runway was approaching too quickly to abort take-off. With one last desperate effort, the Hampden started to rise, but it was too late. It skimmed the top of the boundary fence, struck a corrugated steel Nissen hut sited in the dispersal area, crashed, and caught fire.

Somehow, once again, all four young men got out of the burning plane alive and, even more remarkably, uninjured.

I only learned of these events in later life, thanks entirely to the wonders of the internet. The next part of the story I only discovered weeks before writing this. It came as a shock. There were fatalities on that night: inside the Nissen hut were members of the Scampton ground crew. Three of them were killed. They were Aircraftman R.W. King, Aircraftman W. Fraser, and Aircraftman R. Rennie. Their three families received the devastating news they hoped never to hear.

In some ways, the war was worse for the families waiting at home; they had to live with the constant nagging apprehension that bad news might arrive at any moment while being powerless to prevent it – and there was still the mundane stuff of normal life to deal with. They were helpless onlookers.

Whether or not Arthur told his parents up in Hexham what had happened that night, I don't know. How he and his crew mates dealt with the full, shocking realisation of it can only be guessed. They would have very little time to process their emotions before the next operation. The war went on with ever-increasing intensity.

On the night before Christmas eve, they were sent to attack the German city of Dessau. It was almost as far away as Berlin. Maybe it was impossible to find the target when the Hampden got there, but for some unexplained reason, they were compelled to divert and attack the port city of Emden instead, some 250 miles to the northwest. By the time they were back in the skies above England, the Hampden was approaching the very limit of its range, and fuel was running critically low. Scampton was too far north, so, with near empty tanks, there was no choice but to make a forced landing at the first air base they could find. It had been touch and go, but there would be a Christmas dinner after all.

And so, 1940 drew to a close with Garwell, Flux, Kirke and White still together and halfway through their first tour. What would the New Year bring?

CHAPTER 5

Dicing with Death

Trying to impede the German war effort by bombing military targets from high altitude at night had one major flaw – most of the bombs missed their target.

At the start of the war, Bomber Command had no accurate way of determining the success of its operations; it was up to returning crews to say if a target had been hit or not, and it was hard to be sure from thousands of feet up in the dark. The Air Ministry needed a way of verifying these claims, so by 1941, cameras were being mounted under bombers and automatically triggered when bombs were released. Analysis of the photographic evidence they produced showed just how wrong crew reports had been. Shockingly, it turned out that only 5% of the bombers that set out got within five miles of their target. Half the bombs dropped fell on open countryside. The report that resulted hastened the shift from the attempted precision bombing of military targets to area bombing of German cities.

Wherever the top brass decided to target, the crews, obviously, had no inkling of it until the briefing for that night's raid. By March 1941, Garwell's crew were nearing the completion of their first tour of duty. They had survived the anti-aircraft flak, the fighter attacks, and the crashes on home soil. They had got lost at times, but not hopelessly so, frozen to the bone but avoiding frostbite.

Their luck had held – just.

Saturday 1st March 1941. The target that night was the medieval city of Cologne, with its magnificent gothic Cathedral, situated on the west bank of the river Rhine. It was a heavily defended military command headquarters and a centre of German industry, but also the home to some half a million inhabitants. Bombs were unlikely to fall on open countryside there.

It is the only raid of the thirty in that first tour of duty that I have any details of, thanks to a letter Arthur wrote to his parents on Tuesday 4th March, just three days after the raid. It starts with the more ordinary matters of family life:

'Dear Mum & Dad,

Received your paper and letter today and thank you very much. I was very glad to hear that Mum is doing well under her new treatment. That, combined with the arrival of spring, should soon put you back on your feet again.

I see that someone has put a notice in the Hexham Courant about Uncle Will. It shook me a bit to see it. I can still hardly realise that he has gone.'

Then onto matters of flying – in this case very low over 'Viewlands,' the family home:

'I was pleased you saw me over the other day. I knew that no one was at home – at least I saw no one come outside. I trust that all the snow I saw has now cleared away.'

I'm not sure that this way of checking up on the family was allowed, given that Hexham was 170 miles north of Scampton and in the opposite direction to the usual flight paths, but there was more than a hint of the rule-breaker about Pilot Sergeant Garwell.

And then he describes the raid:

'Things here are cracking along much as usual. Had another do on Cologne the other night – Saturday it must have been. Left it in flames again.

We had a most interesting battle over here with a Jerry long-range fighter. He made three attacks on us from about 20 yards range. It was a pitch-black night and pouring with rain & fortunately, he did not get us, though we collected a few bullets in the tail. My gunners at the back put up a grand show and may have damaged him.

I landed at an aerodrome in Norfolk eventually that night, and who do you think I met but old Curry. You remember him, Dad – he used to go to the Grammar School & played on the wing for Tynedale. He is an observer on night fighters.'

There is something of the 'Boys Own' adventure comic about this description of his brush with death; almost chirpy, upbeat. He wouldn't want to alarm his mum and dad with any expression of fear, but I wonder if the full implication of 'left it in flames again' could have been completely pushed aside. The Hampden had come so close to being shot down; the weather was foul, visibility next to zero, and Kirke, the navigator, couldn't find Scampton - maybe that was enough to be thinking about. There was a job to be done and no choice about doing it beyond point blank refusal - and that was unthinkable.

The same letter then heads off in a different direction:

'We have had a world-famous portrait painter up here to do a life-size picture of some of the squadron being briefed in flying kit. His name is Frank Salisbury R.A. He is supposed to be about the best in the world. He did the Coronation picture and has painted every one of great importance like Roosevelt etc. He did an oil painting of Kirke and me for incorporation into the picture. Made a grand job of it too. Got my hair just right. Everyone whom he paints signs their name in a big book he keeps, so mine went down in the same book as that of the King, the Princesses, Roosevelt & even Benito Mussolini.

With love to my little sister.

Cheerio,

Arthur.'

'Got my hair just right.' – well, it was certainly ginger! Frank Salisbury's preparatory study in oil paint now hangs in my brother's sitting room in Otley, West Yorkshire, so it's easy to judge. The famous wartime painting it came to be part of is called 'The Briefing;' it still hangs to this day in the Officer's Mess at RAF Scampton. Garwell and Kirke, crewmates, stand to the left of a crowded briefing room as others pore over maps laid out on a large table. The ginger mop is unmissable.

At the bottom of the painting, beneath the RAF insignia of a crown and an eagle with outspread wings, there is a quotation from a poem by Stephen Spender:

'Born of the sun, they travelled a short while toward the sun. And left the vivid air signed with their honour.'

Their first tour of duty completed, Garwell, Kirke, Flux, and White had cheated the odds and survived; so many others had not.

The four young crew mates, now friends, left 83 Squadron and went their separate ways. Three of them would meet again before long.

Garwell & Kirke. Preparatory sketch in oils by Frank Salisbury R.A.

CHAPTER 6

Boy Meets Girl

With his first tour of duty completed, Pilot Sergeant Garwell received a commission to the rank of Pilot Officer, was awarded the Distinguished Flying Medal (DFM), and then posted to RAF Finningley. It was April 1941.

Thirty miles northwest of Scampton and four miles from Doncaster, RAF Finningley had, in the previous month, become Operational Training Unit number 25, newly set up to train night bomber crews to fly the Handley Page Hampden. Survive a tour of duty, and the next job was a stint away from combat as an instructor. It was a perfect fit for Garwell but not necessarily a safer occupation.

On the 19th day of the same month, Hampden P1248 took off from Finningley with two crew on board - the trainee pilot and an instructor. It was to be an exercise in instrument-only flying, with the instructor acting as an observer and lookout. The flight commander back at the base had decided that, for some unknown reason, a wireless operator would not be necessary. It was a fatal mistake.

At 16:25 in the afternoon, while flying over Sheffield, the bomber, shrouded in low cloud, veered off the designated route. The pilot and instructor could see nothing, certainly not the steel barrage balloon cable that sliced through the port wing, throwing the aircraft into a spiralling dive. The trainee, Pilot Officer Ralf Allsebrook, scrambled out and parachuted to safety. The instructor, Flying Officer Jeffrey Ranson, did not - another young life cut short. The Hampden smashed into the ground at the edge of Concord Park in the suburbs of Sheffield - close to the present-day Meadowhall Shopping Centre and the M1 motorway.

Had a wireless operator been on board, he would have picked up the warning radio signal emitted by the barrage balloon and averted the disaster. It was a mistake never to be repeated at 25 O.T.U.

Lives so closely shadowed by the prospect of death could take nothing for granted; tomorrow might never arrive. Any brief respite from the threat was to be grasped with both hands. An evening trip to a dance hall in Doncaster was a chance, just for a moment, to re-engage with normal life and let loose. There the men of RAF Finningley could relax, drink, and, best of all, meet girls. Lots of girls.

'Some enchanted evening, you may see a stranger. You may see a stranger across a crowded room.'

Was it like these lyrics from 'South Pacific' when Arthur first saw Joan Shepherd across a Doncaster dance floor? Was it love at first sight? Probably not quite. For while there was plenty to admire about the vivacious girl who first met his eye, Arthur was inexperienced and just a little shy. Piloting a bomber, fine, but wooing a woman? Not so easy. Positively awkward. She could dance brilliantly; he could not. She wore the latest fashions with flair; he wore a uniform. Still, that face, that figure; there was nothing for it but to try.

And what did she see? A slim, handsome RAF Officer with wavy red hair flopping across his forehead, maybe leaning against the bar with a cigarette, a look of studied nonchalance, a slightly raised eyebrow, and a steady gaze. A man's man carefully hiding any inner doubts. A catch.

They talked, they danced, they laughed, they drank, and for all too brief a moment, they forgot the world outside. He walked her home. They agreed to meet again. It was July.

He went back to camp; she went back to the little house in Flowett Street and Blossom. He climbed, yet again, into a bomber's slender fuselage, and she went back to being a dental nurse for Doctor Wallis. *"Is that your young man again?"* Dr Wallis would ask as Arthur's Hampden buzzed low over his new girlfriend's place of work. *"I think so,"* she would say, blushing slightly.

Those nights spent dancing were nights to remember: the band's rhythmic beat, the shimmering shards of light from the glitter ball, the press of young bodies high on excitement, and the possibilities of love. Three summers later, he would write this postcard to Joan from Stalag Luft 3:

> *'Darling – many thanks for your letter of March 3rd, which reached me this morning, taking just three months on the trip… We have been playing some Victor Silvester records tonight & I have felt in the dancing mood all evening. How I wish I had those dainty feet of yours to tread on! And then perhaps a walk in the moonlight. Well, as Van Toen's father always writes, "it must end sometime"!! Very cheering, that! But true! Have had bags of sun lately. Started at 9 am this morning & had to put on my shirt at 2 to stop myself from bursting into flames. Ever yours, darling. Arthur.'*

They met whenever they could. There were walks in the moonlight; there were walks in the rain. They kissed. They became lovers.

But danger was never far away. On August 9th, Arthur wrote this letter to his parents from a bed at the RAF Hospital in Sleaford:

'Dear Family,

You will see that for the moment I have changed my address. I had a slight accident on Thursday afternoon. I wasn't flying either. I was sitting on the back of a lorry with several others, travelling back to the hangers after flying, when we turned a sharp corner, and the side flew out. Four of us went into the road - yours truly on his head. I was knocked out for a short while and was supposed to suffer from concussion, so they sent me here. You see, anyone who flies and has a concussion must have a full medical before he flies again. I shall probably be here for a fortnight and should then get some leave. I feel very well actually but have the most colossal black eye you have ever seen. They thought I had broken my arm, but apparently, it is all right.

My friend Penman was also knocked about a bit. He cut his hand rather badly but has remained at Finningley.

I learn that we are only allowed 20 cigarettes a week here, so I would be very glad if you could send me some as early as possible.'

It must have seemed ironic that he had walked away unscathed from two plane crashes, only for a lorry to put him in a hospital, but he was well enough to worry more about the shortage of cigarettes.

I remember my mother recounting this event many years later –

and also mentioning David Penman, the softly spoken Scot who would, at Arthur's request, accompany her to the dance hall if he couldn't make it, as would have been the case here. She became very fond of Penman, but Arthur was still her man.

His letter home finishes with this:

> *'By the way, since I wrote to you last, I have been trying to get on to Flying Fortresses when I do go back on ops. I may be able to manage it.*
>
> *I think this is all for this morning. The sisters chase me if I sit up for long. Cheerio.*
>
> *Love.*
>
> *Arthur.'*

At the start of the war, the RAF didn't possess a heavy bomber. The Americans did - the Boeing B-17c (dubbed the 'Flying Fortress'). It was a four-engined giant compared to the lowly Hampden. The RAF ordered twenty and first used them in a high-altitude daylight raid on the German port of Wilhelmshaven in July 1941. The experiment failed - they couldn't fly high enough to avoid German fighters, and eight of them were lost within two months. They were withdrawn from operations over Europe soon after, so Arthur's ambition was thwarted - luckily for him.

As summer slipped into autumn, his posting as an instructor at Finningley came to a close. His trainees - 'sprogs' in RAF slang - hadn't killed themselves, or him, and the tired old Hampdens had held together. It was time for some well-earned leave before the next tour of duty and time to introduce Joan to his family up at 'Viewlands.' She felt a flutter of nervousness as they pushed open the little white gate and walked down the garden path to the green-painted back door under its sheltering porch, but they were both welcomed as warmly as the Garwell reserve allowed. She loved it there. He later wrote:

'It *makes me think of that first trip you did up there – when I was fortunate enough to be with you. That was a wizard leave – only far too short.*'

It was, and when it ended, they headed away, she to Doncaster and he to his new posting with 44 'Rhodesia' Squadron at RAF Waddington, five miles south of Lincoln. He waved goodbye to his sweetheart, but it was goodbye to the Hampden bombers as well; their days in Bomber Command would soon be over. A much bigger and more potent weapon awaited him - something brand new.

Half of the 1,432 Hampdens built for the RAF were lost on operations, with 1,077 men killed and 739 reported as missing. Enemy action accounted for 237 aircraft, and 214 just went missing, cause unknown. 33 crashed on take-off, 30 crashed at sea, and 23 were abandoned in mid-air. 175 crashed on land, often with their crews still inside. They littered the fields, woods, and villages of Lincolnshire and beyond, smashing into churches, ripping into cottages, tearing up hedgerows, and toppling trees. Young bodies burned, broken, and destroyed; countless future generations dying with them.

Arthur and his crew were among the lucky ones; they had survived their 30 missions. On the 4th of November 1941,

Arthur, accompanied by his parents, attended an investiture at Buckingham Palace and was decorated with the Distinguished Flying Medal by the King.

CHAPTER 7

News from Malaya

Joan Shepherd wheeled her white bicycle out of the backyard of Blossom's little house on Flowitt Street and set off for Dr Wallis's dental surgery and another day at work. It was late December 1941, and she was wrapped up against the cold, damp air. Rounding a corner, she could just make out the figure of a blond-haired young man walking along the wet pavement some way ahead. Her brother Peter! It must be, but no, it couldn't be – he was thousands of miles away in the Far East. It was like the fleeting, mistaken recognition of a loved one by someone recently bereaved, but Peter Shepherd wasn't dead. Not quite.

At the outbreak of war and in a rush to mobilise men as quickly as possible, his RAF apprenticeship had been suddenly shortened from three years to two. Once completed, he was deemed to be a fully qualified aero-engine fitter even though he was just a boy of seventeen. Some months later, in August 1941, he was put on a ship for a nine-week journey to Singapore. Sailing away from war-torn Britain didn't seem so bad, especially as Southeast Asia had not yet been touched by the war. Malaya was then a valuable part of the British Empire and, with an increasingly hostile Japan close by, had to be protected, so RAF bases were being hastily set up to counter the perceived threat.

From Singapore, Peter was put on a train for a 400-mile journey up the Malayan peninsula to a place called Sungai Petani. There, in a clearing carved out of a rubber plantation, he found a makeshift airfield, a few wooden huts with corrugated iron roofs, a control tower of sorts, and very little else. It was like another world.

He was posted to maintain the aircraft of No. 27 Squadron, which operated twelve Bristol Blenheim light bombers. The steamy heat and humidity of Malaya did nothing for the already modest performance of these aircraft, plus the frequent torrential rains could, at their worst, render the grass airstrip unusable for days on end. Spare parts were in short supply. It was all a bit ramshackle.

His life in camp settled into an easy-going and frequently boring routine; many long afternoons were spent sheltering from the raging thunderstorms of monsoon season with rain hammering down on the tin roofs of the huts for hours on end. If there was a threat of aggression from Japan, no one seemed to be taking it very seriously. At times it felt like he had been dumped in Sungai Petani and forgotten.

By early December, the mood had changed; leave passes were cancelled, and rumours of troop movements and a 'state of readiness' circulated, although nothing official filtered down to the lower ranks. Tensions rose, but the airfield remained eerily quiet. Everything looked normal.

At 1 am on Monday 8th December, Peter, still in his oil-stained overalls after working on a Blenheim's engines until midnight, fell into his bed exhausted. Moonlight flooded the open window of his hut, the silence of the night punctuated by the occasional rustling of some nocturnal creature in the trees and the distant low throb of a generator. He fell asleep, and the hours passed unnoticed.

The noise that woke him was sudden, loud, and repetitive. In his sleep-drugged state, it was hard to decipher, but it sounded like a series of rapid explosions coming from the airfield, each one getting nearer and ever louder. Gripped by fear and realising that the detonations were heading his way, he jumped off the bed and wedged himself between it and the wall, clutching his head in his hands and closing his eyes. The next explosion was massive and very close by; one more, and that would be it. He waited in horror for only an instant before it came, and his world turned black.

When Peter's eyes next opened, he was lying on his back staring up at a pale dawn sky and slowly drifting dark-grey smoke. He was no longer in his room; there were no walls around him and no ceiling above. He tried to move but couldn't, and as the numbing shock gradually receded, an excruciating pain enveloped him. He tried to cry out, but his pitifully weak voice was lost in a vast, silent emptiness. Time crept by. Then, suddenly, a sweat-stained face peered down at him; *"There's one over here!"* the young airman shouted. Another airman joined him, his face pale with fear. They both looked down at the prone, twisted body in front of them, but then, in a moment, they were gone.

Drifting in and out of consciousness, it was impossible to tell how long it was before they returned with a stretcher, but it seemed like a lifetime. One lifted his shoulders and the other his feet in such a way that his back bent in the middle. He screamed in agony and passed out. When he came to, they were lowering the stretcher onto the wooden floor of the sick bay. They tried to lift him again. He passed out with the pain again. He was next aware of laying on a bed in the sick bay where two orderlies were frantically tending to a lad in the next bed who he knew as one of the airframe fitters. One of this young man's legs ended in a tangle of shattered bone and sinew above where his knee should have been. They were trying to stem the flow of blood with a tourniquet.

And the cause of this carnage? Without declaring war, the Japanese had launched an all-out bombing offensive against British air bases in Malaya, destroying some 60 Allied aircraft on the first day, injuring and killing many servicemen. They simultaneously carried out the infamous attack on the United States naval base at Pearl Harbour, Hawaii, sinking four battleships, destroying 188 aircraft, and killing over 2,000 men. It brought the United States into World War II.

For Joan's eighteen-year-old brother, it was the start of a long and painful journey; at first to a town two hundred miles to the south called Johor Bahru – a train journey of some seven hours in the company of other horribly injured servicemen. There, in a newly built hospital, his injuries could be properly assessed and treated: there were many, including fractures to the jaw, elbow, ankle, pelvis, and the base of the spine. He was unable to urinate without a catheter, and his bowels seemed to have stopped working. His condition deteriorated, and when, one night, he started to pass blood, he was rushed to the operating theatre for emergency surgery, waking the next morning to find a rubber tube protruding from his abdomen and a priest sitting by his bed; neither of them good signs.

A few days later, on Boxing Day, he was told by the matron that a telegram had been sent to his father back in England to say that his son had been injured and was in a critical condition. That's how Joan knew. The little brother she had tried to protect from school bullies was now beyond her reach and, for all she knew, close to death. Was she to lose Peter as well as her baby sister June? She would hear no more news until March the following year, the agony of not knowing his fate constantly playing on her mind.

By the second week of January, the haemorrhaging crisis had passed, but Peter was still riddled with infection and unable to eat. His days were spent drifting in and out of a drugged sleep while the Japanese ground forces pushed relentlessly down the Malayan peninsula towards the hospital where he lay in Johor Bahru and Singapore Island just beyond it.

On 18th January 1942, at midnight, he was moved by ambulance to Singapore General Hospital, where the wards were so crammed with the injured that mattresses had to be laid on the floor to try and accommodate the almost continual stream of new arrivals, including civilians. The fetid air of the wards reverberated to the sound of explosions and anti-aircraft guns as the Japanese pressed home air attacks on the nearby harbour. On top of that, morphine supplies had all but run out. It was chaos.

Three weeks later, on 13th February, Peter was evacuated on a barely sea-worthy riverboat for a two-week journey to the island of Java. Two days after he left, Singapore fell to the Japanese. It was the largest British military surrender in history, with some 80,000 troops taken prisoner, many of whom died in captivity.

From Java, Peter was taken by hospital ship to Karachi in what was then British India. It would be a year before he was well enough to be discharged. When he finally arrived back in Britain to convalesce, his RAF career was at an end.

Arthur's letter to Joan dated 29th July 1944 includes this comment:

'You sounded a little worried about Peter in one of your letters. I'm sure he will be fine when he has settled down in his civilian occupation. You know it is a very big change to go from service life into an office. Most people here don't like the idea much – and just as after the last war, people are keen to get away from what seems too artificial a life.'

But Joan continued to worry - it was in her nature.

CHAPTER 8

Turning Points

The town of Amesbury sits by the river Avon at the southern edge of Salisbury plain, near where the A303 swoops past the ancient monument of Stonehenge. On its eastern edge, at Boscombe Down, is the longest military runway in the country; it's where the Ministry of Defence tests and evaluates military aircraft. In 1941 it was called the Aeroplane and Armament Experimental Establishment.

In November 1941, the RAF drew together some of its most experienced bomber crews at Boscombe Down to learn how to fly the first production models of a completely new heavy bomber, the Avro Lancaster Mk1. They were referred to as the 'Intensive Flying (Lancaster) Flight.' Pilot Officer Garwell, newly posted to 44 Squadron, was among their number, and it was there that he first met John Dering Nettleton. Although from very different backgrounds, they seemed to click.

Born in South Africa and the grandson of a Royal Navy Admiral, the quietly spoken Nettleton, three years older than Garwell, had joined the RAF as a commissioned officer in December 1938. He was tall, dark-haired, and handsome, with the sort of cut-glass accent beloved of the English upper classes. As the war progressed, he proved himself to be a natural leader and rose through the ranks rapidly. He was soon to become a squadron leader at RAF

Waddington, charged with seeing the new bomber into service.

It was impossible not to be impressed by the menacing presence of this new and still secret weapon. The Lancaster dwarfed the Hampden in every way: length, height, wingspan, weight, and armament. With its four Rolls Royce Merlin V12 supercharged engines, it could fly faster, further, and at higher altitudes while carrying a much heavier bomb load. It would mark a turning point in the RAF's war effort.

On 24th December, Christmas Eve, the Avro Lancaster was declared ready for service. Seven aircraft left A.V. Roe's factory in Chadderton - near Oldham in Lancashire - for delivery to 44 Squadron at RAF Waddington. They were the first of over 7,000 Lancasters that were eventually built.

On 3rd January, Arthur wrote to Joan to say that he was leaving Boscombe Down to return to Waddington:

'Dear Joan,

Just a brief note to let you know that I am on the move again. I now have to go back to Waddington and expect to make the trip tomorrow. You had better address your letters to the Officer's Mess, RAF Waddington, Lincs.

It's a rather good thing, isn't it, dear? It means that from now on, we shall see a good deal more of each other.

I received your letter written on New Year's Eve this morning. I am looking forward with some interest to the time when I do come and see you and you prove to me that you do love me!

I'm afraid I haven't much more to tell you today, darling. Everything's a bit mixed up, so I will just say cheerio.

All my love to you.

Arthur.'

Things may have been *'a bit mixed up'* as to what awaited him at RAF Waddington, but there was obviously more on his mind than just being a bomber pilot.

As it happened, he didn't make the trip the following day as expected, and he didn't go straight back to Waddington. On January 18th (by coincidence, the very same day that the injured Peter Shepherd was transferred to Singapore hospital), he was sent to the Rolls Royce factory in Derby, where the Lancaster's mighty Merlin engines were being manufactured. He was there for a week, seeing their production first-hand, before travelling back to Waddington on the 25th.

Now it was time for the pilots of 44 Squadron to get to grips with how to fly the new aircraft, no doubt helped by those that had returned from Boscombe Down. Inevitably there were teething problems: Squadron Leader Nettleton lost a tailwheel after hitting a pile of frozen snow on the runway; others ran out of the runway just before they managed to stop. Various bits dropped off in flight, including, on one occasion, an engine, but a Lancaster could easily be flown with the remaining three. It was a tough old bird.

'Ginger' Garwell was not immune to such mishaps: on the 13th of February, a week after his 22nd birthday, he was piloting one of the newly delivered Lancasters on a training flight heading for RAF Thornaby in North Yorkshire. Unusually, the crew had been joined by a civilian passenger, an employee of a company connected with the war effort. It would have been an exciting, if not scary, experience for a civilian, but the aircraft landed safely, and all was well.

All was not so well when, later in the day, Garwell and crew attempted take-off for a return to Waddington. For some unknown reason, the Lancaster left the runway and ran into a barbed wire fence on the perimeter of the airfield. There was no serious damage, and Lancaster L7533 was soon returned to service, but it must have brought back dark memories of the fatal accident in the Hampden just over a year earlier.

Less than two months later, on 9th May, and with a different crew, Lancaster L7533 was lost without trace on an operation to bomb the German port of Warnemunde. The crew was recorded as missing.

Despite the mishaps, all agreed that the Lancaster was a vast improvement on everything that had gone before.

In the same month as the incident at Thornaby, there was another major turning point for the RAF: the arrival of a new Commander-in-Chief at Bomber Command – a man who would become, by the end of the war, notorious.

When Air Marshall Sir Arthur Travers Harris first arrived at Bomber Command's HQ in High Wycombe, a directive from the Air Ministry was already sitting on his desk. Headed 'Area Bombing Directive,' it had the full approval of Churchill's War Cabinet. The previous strategy of targeting military and manufacturing installations with so-called 'precision bombing' had met with abject failure, so there were new instructions:

> *'The primary object of your operations should now be focused on the morale of the enemy civilian population and, in particular, of the industrial workers.'*

This meant the bombing and burning of German cities with all the horror that would inevitably entail. Arthur Harris, a bullish, battle-hardened veteran of the First World War, would prove to be utterly ruthless in the pursuit of this objective. In his words:

> *"The Nazis entered this war under the rather childish delusion that they were going to bomb everyone else, and nobody was going to bomb them… they sowed the wind, and now they are going to reap the whirlwind."*

And later:

> *"We are going to scourge the Third Reich from end to end. We are bombing Germany city by city and ever more terribly in order to make it impossible for her to go on with the war. That is our object; we shall pursue it relentlessly."*

He earned the nickname 'Bomber Harris.'

Events were moving quickly: on the 3rd of March, Waddington crews carried out their first operation with the newly arrived Lancasters, a mine-laying mission in the North Sea aimed at German shipping routes. It was known in the RAF as 'gardening.' The aircraft's performance far exceeded expectations; it opened up new possibilities - ones that 'Bomber' Harris would exploit at the earliest opportunity.

As for 'Ginger' Garwell, luck still seemed to be on his side: he was reunited with two of his old 83 Squadron crewmates from Scampton; his wireless operator, Flight Sergeant Robert 'Bob' Flux, and his navigator/observer, Warrant Officer Frank Kirke - the New Zealander who had posed with him for the painting by Frank Salisbury. Like Garwell, both of them had earned the Distinguished Flying Medal after their first tour of duty at

Scampton. Little did they know then that their war would be over before spring was out.

Four friends from 44 Squadron.
Photo courtesy of the RAF Waddington Heritage Centre.
L-R: D. Appleton, Flying Officer Ball DFC,
Flight Lieutenant Hall DFC, Flying Officer Garwell DFM.

CHAPTER 9

Something's Afoot

When instructions arrived from RAF HQ for crews to come off operations and start practicing daylight formation flying, the rumours started. Why do that when almost all raids were carried out at night when formation flying was impossible? Guesswork abounded, none of it particularly credible. Still, flying over British soil had to be a safer option than engaging the enemy - for as long as it might last.

It didn't come easy at first, but as the routes got longer and the formations tighter, confidence grew. Three Lancasters in a V-shaped formation followed closely behind by another three, making six in all, with two more tagging along on their flanks as reserves. It was becoming obvious that something big was in the offing and that, whatever it was, it would be in daylight. All crews were sworn to secrecy.

Squadron Leader Nettleton led the first formation for 44, with Sergeant George Rhodes flying to the right in the number two position and Flying Officer Garwell to the left. Behind them, Flight Lieutenant Reginald Sandford led the second formation with Warrant Officer John Beckett to his left and Warrant Officer Hubert Crum to his right - both holders of the Distinguished Flying Medal.

Meanwhile, at Woodhall Spa, a few miles East of Waddington, 97 Squadron was practising the same daylight formation flying without knowing that both squadrons were destined for the same mission. Leading the second section for them was none other than twenty-three-year-old Flight Lieutenant David Penman, Joan Shepherd's stand-in dance partner. He had already won a Distinguished Flying Cross during his first tour with 44 Squadron.

Each Lancaster carried a crew of seven. The pilot had the most comfortable seat, cushioned and adjustable with an armour-plated backrest. To the right of him, the co-pilot sat on a folding bench with a more rudimentary backrest of detachable webbing. The bomb-aimer accessed his position in the lower Perspex bubble of the nose compartment via a downward step in front of the co-pilot's seat, which had to be dismantled for the purpose. There, when the time came, he would lay face down with a clear view of the ground and the bomb release trigger in his hand. Either side of his head were the boots of the front gunner who stood in the upper turret to operate two Browning .303 machine guns. The observer, who doubled up as the bomb aimer and navigator, sat at a desk behind the pilot's seat, a lamp illuminating his charts and instruments. Behind him sat the wireless operator. That left two more men, the upper and rear gunners. Reaching their positions involved scrambling over the main wing spar and down the narrowing fuselage through the dark, exposed guts of the aircraft. The upper gunner then clambered into his clear Perspex turret, leaving his parachute stowed nearby and hoping it would never be needed - not that it would be of any use in a low-level raid. The rear gunner pressed on, over the tailplane spar and down to the far end of the aircraft, where he had to scramble feet-first into the rear four-gun turret, closing and locking the sliding doors behind him. It was the loneliest position of all.

On April 15th, 1942, it was time for 44 Squadron's final practice flight; if no one had much of a clue as to what was in store before, the penny was starting to drop now. From Lincolnshire, they were to head for the South coast at Selsey Bill, then turn back up country to Lincoln and on to Inverness in Scotland, swooping in to make a simulated bombing run before turning south again, dropping some practise bombs on a target area in the North Sea and returning to base. It was a round trip of some 1,260 miles at low level and required massive concentration; if the lead Lancaster made a mistake and hit something, those following had little to no chance of taking any avoiding action. All returned safely if exhausted. Not much longer to wait now.

The night before the final briefing was a tense affair; the crews were confined to camp, banned from using the telephone, and, worse still, excluded from the bar. Up in Doncaster, Joan Shepherd had no idea what Arthur and his pal David Penman were up to.

At 11 am on Friday the 17th of April, the airmen at Waddington and Woodhall Spa crowded into their respective briefing rooms. All was about to be revealed. On the wall in front of them was a large, brightly lit map of Europe, and on it a length of ribbon which traced a route over occupied France, across Germany, and on to the target, Augsburg, a city deep in Southern Bavaria.

Really? In daylight? At a low level?

It is said that some men gasped while others laughed, thinking it must be some sort of joke. Any of the usual targets, the Ruhr, the ports, even Berlin, maybe, but this seemed off the scale of probability. Why there?

The explanation, when it came, was matter-of-fact and detailed: Augsburg may have been a jewel of renaissance architecture and one of Germany's oldest cities, but on its northern outskirts lay the sprawling factory of M.A.N. (an abbreviation of Maschinenfabrik Augsburg-Nürnberg) where the huge diesel engines that powered Nazi U-boats were being manufactured. Dr Rudolph Diesel had invented his radical new engine some fifty years earlier and M.A.N. in Augsburg, his home city, was the first company to bring it into production. A lifelong pacifist, he couldn't have envisaged the use it was now being put to, sinking millions of tons of Allied shipping in the battle of the Atlantic. Destroying the factory would severely disrupt the building of new U-boats. Only the new Lancaster, with its vastly improved capability, could make such an exploit remotely viable. It was called 'Operation Margin.'

There were detailed maps showing the run-up to the target, even a scale model of the whole complex, including the exact assembly shed that had to be hit. They were told that the factory's defences would be light because it was thought to be too far away for an attack from the air. To draw away the attention of the Luftwaffe's fighters, there would be diversionary raids by RAF Boston bombers on coastal targets in Northern France, supported by as many British fighter planes as could be mustered. The Lancasters would sneak in unnoticed, hugging the ground and thwarting enemy radar detection - or so it was hoped.

At the end of it all, there was nothing more for the Squadron Commander to say but *"Good luck, chaps."* The assembled airmen walked out of the briefing room into the white light of a spring day in almost complete silence and, lost in their own thoughts, headed off to lunch. For thirty-eight of them, it would be the last meal of their young lives.

CHAPTER 10

Hedge-hopping

Just before 3 pm in the afternoon, Arthur Garwell climbed high up into the cabin of Lancaster KM-A and settled into his seat with Laurence Dando, his Rhodesian co-pilot, next to him. Just behind them were his close friends from 83 Squadron days, Frank Kirke, the observer, and Bob Flux, the wireless operator. Their mutual trust after so many close encounters with death was absolute. James Watson took up his position in the front gun turret while, back down the fuselage, a Canadian, Douglas McAlpine, stowed his parachute and squeezed into the mid-upper turret. At the far end of the Lancaster, the length of a cricket pitch away, Ivor Edwards, a young Welshman, slid the doors of his gun turret tightly shut behind him and waited in tense anticipation.

One by one, the Merlin engines of all eight Lancasters roared into life in a deafening crescendo of sound. There were no malfunctions, so one reserve Lancaster shut down its engines and watched the other seven take up a position at the end of the runway while, simultaneously, seven aircraft of 97 Squadron at Woodhall Spa did the same.

They took to the air individually, each with a full fuel load of petrol and four 1,000 lb bombs slung below. The plan was for the two squadrons to join up in the skies above Grantham and head for the south coast together, but Nettleton, leading 44, and

Sherwood, leading 97, missed each other, so the two formations pressed on into the afternoon sunshine on slightly different courses, with, it would turn out, fatal consequences.

At 4:15 pm, above the coast at Selsey Bill, 44's reserve Lancaster turned for home as the remaining six headed out across the English Channel, barely skimming the waves below. Meanwhile, twelve Boston bombers, with an escort of Spitfire fighters, launched one of the planned diversionary raids, dropping their bombs on German ships moored in Cherbourg harbour. It succeeded in drawing eighteen Messerschmitt 109 fighters into battle, diverting their attention from the approaching Lancasters. A short time later, another twelve Bostons launched raids to the east, bringing even more German fighters into the fray. Some seventy Spitfires kept them fully engaged in battle and then, suddenly, withdrew. The timing had been almost perfect.

Thirty minutes later, at 4:44 pm, Nettleton's formation slipped unnoticed across the French coast near Deauville and altered course, heading for a point south of Paris. The 97 Squadron formation, led by Squadron Leader Sherwood, crossed shortly after on a slightly different course but convinced that theirs was the more accurate. There were six hundred miles still to fly to reach the target.

At a speed of one hundred and eighty miles an hour and hugging the contours of the ground as closely as they dared, Nettleton's formation passed over the sleepy villages and verdant farmland of Normandy like a shockwave, skimming the tops of trees. Horses and cattle fled in terror at the deafening noise of twenty-four Merlin engines in full flight. Upturned French faces looked briefly skyward before ducking for cover. A few, recognising Allied aircraft, had just enough time to wave. Hedge-hopping, it was called, and it shook the roof tiles of every house in its path.

Passing close to the town of Lisieux, just eighteen miles from the coast, a hail of fire from a hidden flak battery hit one of the Lancasters in 44's second section and knocked out four of its six Browning machine guns - a stark warning of what lay ahead.

Then, some fifty miles inland, Nettleton's formation flew a little too close to a Luftwaffe air base at Beaumont-le-Roger just as some thirty Messerschmitt 109 and Focke-Wulf 190 fighters were returning from an abortive mission to intercept one of the RAF's diversionary raids at Rouen. As the fighters swooped in to land, one of the pilots thought he saw something moving rapidly on the horizon. Looking harder, he caught a glimpse of three bombers in the distance, followed by three more, their black hulks silhouetted against the late afternoon sky. Instinctively he opened the throttle, retracted the landing gear, and headed back up, simultaneously alerting his fellow pilots who were some way behind him. They all followed suit.

What happened next is recorded in great detail in many later accounts - in particular a book by the late Jack Currie DFC called 'The Augsburg Raid.' It was the start of a running battle that could never be on equal terms. The Luftwaffe fighters closed in on Nettleton's formation like a pack of hyenas closing in on slower prey, attacking the most vulnerable first - and that was the already damaged V-Victor piloted by Warrant Officer Joseph Beckett. A hail of cannon fire hit one of the engines, which immediately burst into flames. The inferno spread rapidly, consuming the

Lancaster's vitals and enveloping the fuel tanks. V-Victor dropped back, crippled and in its death throes. It ploughed into the ground, hit a stand of trees, and disintegrated into a fireball. There were no survivors.

The German pilot who claimed that 'kill' was Hauptmann (Captain) Hiene Greisert. Meeting in other circumstances, at other times, these airmen of the Luftwaffe and the RAF might have shared a drink and swapped stories. There would have been mutual respect for each other's skills and bravery and, no doubt, laughter. But not now - not when the war pitched them against each other in deadly combat.

In the second section of Nettleton's formation, Warrant Officer Hubert 'Bert' Crum, piloting Lancaster T-Tommy, guessed that he would be the next target for the swarming German fighters. Like his close friend Beckett, he was a hardened survivor of many missions and, also like Beckett, tough and clear-thinking. He didn't have long to wait. A hail of cannon fire ripped into the fuselage of T-Tommy, catching the port wing on fire. In the ensuing chaos, Crum remained calm; he lowered the bomb flaps and shouted amid the din for the bombs to be set on safe and jettisoned. As 4,000 lbs of high explosives dropped harmlessly into the fields below, the Lancaster lurched briefly upwards before heading for the ground. Crum held her as steady as he could while Bert Dowty, manning the front gun turret, braced himself for the inevitable, terrifying impact. Finding a stretch of land unencumbered by trees, Crum gently nursed 30 tons of burning aircraft, wheels up, into the soft, unsuspecting grass, where it eventually ground to a shuddering halt. All the crew, bar one, scrambled out. Bert Dowty, stuck in the front turret, was desperately trying, and failing, to smash his way out with the muzzle of his Browning machine gun. Seeing his plight, Crum attacked the Perspex with a crash-axe until Dowty was freed. Once satisfied that fire would destroy what was still a secret weapon, they all made for the cover of nearby woodland with the hope of making their escape. It would be a very long time before they tasted freedom again.

There was now only one Lancaster left of 44's second section, P-Peter, piloted by Flight Lieutenant Reginald 'Nick' Sandford, a Londoner from Twickenham. It is said that he always wore his pyjamas under his flying suit for luck, but with three German fighters locked onto the Lancaster's tail, the lucky pyjamas seemed to be failing him. He could just make out a line of high-tension electricity cables directly ahead and faced a sudden choice - fly over or under? Instinctively he took the huge bomber even closer to the ground and, with consummate skill, flew underneath them. The predatory Bf 109's followed with ease, knowing that their relentless cannon fire would soon bring the lumbering beast down. With all four engines now ablaze and the fuselage shredded, the Lancaster's end was sudden and catastrophic; it hit the ground and exploded on impact, instantly killing all seven young airmen.

The pilot who fired the final, fatal, salvo was Unteroffizier Pohl, and for him and the Jagdgeschwader 2 'Richthofen' fighter wing, it was to be a cause of great celebration - it was their one thousandth 'kill.'

There may be few more poignant illustrations of the opposing fortunes of war than the letter that Sandford's co-pilot, a young Rhodesian, Pilot Officer 'Buster' Peall, had written to his mother just days before the raid. He had left it inside his locker back at base – just in case. It started like this:

'My darling Mother, I knew from the start that this was bound to happen in the end, and I have always thought that my only regret would be not saying thank you and goodbye. It seems strange writing so, but I feel I must. I will not begin to thank you for everything because words cannot express it, and anyway, it would take far too long. Like Dad, I am not afraid to die but just don't want to. But 'God's will be done,' so instead of coming home to you, I go and meet Dad.'

Nettleton, concentrating intensely on what lay ahead, had not witnessed the horror that had befallen the three crews in his second section. His gunners had seen it all and conveyed the desperate news over the crackling intercom. So now they were down to three; Nettleton in B-Baker with Garwell to his left in A-Apple and Rhodes to his right in H-Howe. They were the next targets.

By this time, the attackers had worked out that these new bombers were armed with machine guns that lacked the range of the Messerschmitt's cannons. It could never be a fair fight. The Lancaster's guns had one other flaw; they were prone to jamming. On H-Howe, every single gun had jammed and was useless. It was a sitting duck.

Major Walter Oesau, the Commander of the fighter unit and an ace with a hundred victories to his name, could see the plight of Rhodes' aircraft and closed in from behind. With no more need to keep a safe distance, the end was inevitable; a sustained burst of fire tore into the defenceless Lancaster with deadly accuracy.

What happened next has never been properly understood; instead of heading for the ground, H-Howe climbed violently upwards until it could climb no more. For a moment, it hung in the air directly above Nettleton and Garwell, and then it stalled. To the watching crews below, it seemed to be happening in slow-motion, almost like a film. And then, suddenly, it fell - like a mighty tree might fall between two others with just inches to spare. Hitting the ground nose-first, it disappeared from view in a ball of flame and flying debris. Survival was impossible.

And now there were two. Orders given at the briefing were that if one aircraft in a section was lost early in the flight, the rest of that section should return to base. The orders were ignored.

Nettleton and Garwell pressed on. There was little choice. Bits of A-Apple's shot-up starboard wing flapped like rags in a hurricane as the attackers continued their relentless pursuit. Shots that missed the Lancasters could be seen blowing holes in the houses and villages below. It couldn't last much longer. Then, while pulling away from a close-range attack, the Messerschmitt piloted by Underoffizier Edelmann came within range of Garwell's front gunner, James Watson. He didn't miss. Edelmann landed his damaged aircraft in a field. His aircraft was the one and only German casualty of the whole battle.

Finally, with fuel and ammunition running out, the Messerschmitts were forced to turn back. It was over. The time was 5:15 pm. Twenty-one RAF crew were dead, and seven were on the run somewhere in France.

CHAPTER 11

Augsburg

It was just before 8 pm on a pleasant, sunny evening in old Augsburg, and the annual folk festival was in full swing. Fairground attractions vied with brass bands as the beer flowed and people danced in the mediaeval streets. The war seemed too far away to be much of a worry, but that was about to change – suddenly and dramatically.

Flying east across France, across the German border, and on into Bavaria, all the while closely hugging the contours of the land, Nettleton and Garwell were nearing their target. It looked to German observers like they were headed for Munich, but on reaching Lake Ammersee, they swung hard to the left, found the river they were looking for, and followed it north towards Augsburg.

By now, the gun batteries on the roofs of the M.A.N. Diesel works to the north of the city were manned and ready. Sirens echoed around the narrow streets and squares. Revellers looked up curiously, disbelievingly; what could it be? The answer came with the suddenness of a thunderclap as the two Lancasters roared into view just above the ancient rooftops.

Travelling at almost 200 miles an hour, there was little time for Nettleton and Garwell to locate the factory, but there it was, just beyond the tall chimney stacks that stood directly in their path.

Making a split-second change of direction to avoid a collision, they were now in the line of fire of the rooftop gunners. Flak shells burst all around the two Lancasters as both pilots and bomb-aimers strained to recognise the exact shed they had to hit if this whole crazy enterprise was not to be in vain. It was as they made their final approach with bomb doors open and just seconds to go that Bob Flux in A-Apple shouted above the mayhem, *"We're on fire, Skipper."* The number two and number four engines were ablaze. Garwell glanced round to see a wall of orange flame deep within the fuselage. He ordered his old friend to slam shut the armoured fire doors at the rear of the cabin - it was all that could be done. Frank Kirke, lying face down in the bomb aimer's Perspex bubble, tightened his fingers on the release trigger and pressed. As the four 1,000 lb bombs with eleven-second fuses were released, A-Apple, relieved of their weight, lurched upwards and away from the factory and from the city, its mission accomplished.

The next part of the story I remember from early childhood just as my mother told it to me: the cabin of Dad's aircraft began to fill with choking black smoke as the fire behind the steel doors raged unchecked. He was going to have to bring her down. The five men in the cabin could barely breathe, and the smoke was so thick that they were flying towards the ground blind. Garwell ordered Bob Flux to throw open the escape hatch in the canopy above his head. The rush of cold, clean air cleared the smoke just long enough for him to see what lay a few hundred feet ahead; a park with children playing and beyond it, a line of tall trees. Garwell pulled back on the stick and raised the nose of the dying Lancaster just enough to clear the park and the trees. Then, as the blinding smoke closed in again, he eased her down, unsighted, toward the open land beyond. This was the critical moment.

She slammed belly-first into the soft earth at not much short of 100 miles an hour with an impact so great that the fire-ravaged fuselage broke in half before the shattered aircraft slid to a halt. Finally, five hours after leaving Waddington on that April afternoon, Lancaster R5510 lay still. Four young men scrambled out of the cabin, coughing violently, still barely able to see. My father, Lawrence Dando, James Watson, and Frank Kirke gulped in the fresh Bavarian air and looked around them. Where was Bob Flux? He had been with them a moment before. The answer, when it came, was deeply shocking; the man who had stood up to open the hatch, the man who had likely saved their lives, lay beneath the starboard wing, dead.

My mother didn't try to soften the impact of this on my young imagination; *"He was thrown out of the open hatch and chopped in half by a propeller,"* she said.

There was no sign of Douglas McAlpine or Ivor Edwards. Both of their gun turrets had been consumed by the fire. They stood no chance.

The four shocked survivors were soon surrounded by a swarm of German soldiers. There was nowhere to run, so they stood still and held their hands up. The commanding officer, pistol outstretched, demanded to know who the pilot was. Garwell stepped forward, expecting to be shot on the spot, but instead, the soldier saluted, shook his hand, and said, *"The English, they are gentlemen."* Why? It seems the soldier knew that the easiest place to down the burning Lancaster would have been the park, where, on that sunny afternoon, local children were playing. Instead, the crippled aircraft had been coaxed to the open countryside beyond, saving many innocent lives.

Nettleton and crew, their bombs dropped on target, had seen it all; they had seen the submarine engine manufacturing shed explode as they headed away, and they had seen Garwell's burning Lancaster nearing its end. It is said that my father threw a two-fingered gesture in their direction as they passed, which is wholly believable. They were now alone in the evening twilight with six hundred miles still to fly. As darkness fell, Nettleton coaxed the damaged Lancaster up to high altitude and made for home.

I remember watching a documentary about the raid, which was made for television in the nineteen eighties and narrated by Jack Currie. Even knowing the outcome, it was like watching my own fate hanging by the thinnest thread. How did any of them survive? Toward the end, they interviewed a German citizen, Karl-Heinz Meinecke, who clearly remembered, as a young lad, seeing my father's blazing Lancaster flying overhead. He'd jumped on his bicycle and made for the crash scene, arriving to find the four RAF men standing in a field with a fifth laid in the grass nearby. He was there when soldiers arrived to arrest them.

Not long after the single surviving Lancaster of 44 Squadron had gone, the first three Lancasters of 97 Squadron, led by John Sherwood, roared over the city toward the already burning factory. They had avoided the German fighter planes but now faced the full fury of Augsburg's gunners, who were ready to throw everything they had at them. Faced with a wall of exploding flak, they accelerated up and over the towering chimneys that stood in their way and tore into the target like some unholy trinity,

Rodley, and Hallows clinging in tight formation to Sherwood's tail as the bomb-aimers shouted their final instructions amid the chaos. There was no time for fear. With bombs gone, they dropped almost to street level to try and get under the flak but then Sherwood's Lancaster was hit. It was a fuel tank. Within seconds the fuselage caught fire. Rodley, Hallows, and their crews looked on helplessly as the crippled aircraft dropped back, hit the ground, and exploded. By some miracle, Sherwood was thrown out of the cabin on impact while still strapped to his seat and had his fall broken by the branches of a tree. He was the lone survivor.

And then, finally, the last section began its approach, led by Joan Shepherd's occasional dance partner, David Penman, with Deverill and Mycock flying by his side at two and three. The German defences, now having all their guns trained on the Lancaster's line of approach, let loose with the most ferocious and accurate barrage yet. With over a mile still to go, both Mycock and Deverill's aircraft had been hit; one trailed a mass of flames from its port wing, the other from a starboard engine. They could have turned away and attempted a crash-landing, but they chose not to. By the time they reached the factory, Mycock's Lancaster was a ball of flames. Seconds after releasing its bombs, it exploded in mid-air.

Penman, bombs gone, pulled up and away from the diesel engine works with Deverill, one of his engines still on fire, close behind. Ginger Garwell, standing by the smouldering wreck of his stricken Lancaster, saw them pass and waved. It was over.

Nettleton and his crew got back, finally breaking radio silence to request navigational assistance only to learn that they had overshot

England and were out over the Irish Sea. Turning around, they landed the bullet-ridden aircraft at Squire's Gate aerodrome, near Blackpool, the sole surviving Lancaster of the six that set out from 44 Squadron at Waddington. Rodley, Hallows, Penman, Deverill, and their crews all made it safely back to 97 Squadron at Woodhall Spa, landing their own badly damaged aircraft just before midnight. Deverill's crew had managed to extinguish the fire that had threatened to bring them down, and, luckily, they saw no sign of enemy fighters in the night skies over Germany and France. Just as well, as all their guns had jammed.

Although 38 young men had died and 11 were missing, the top brass back home were keen to proclaim the Augsburg raid a success. The Prime Minister, Winston Churchill, wrote:

> *'Undeterred by heavy losses at the outset, 44 and 97 pierced in broad daylight into the heart of Germany and struck a vital point with deadly precision. We must plainly regard the attack as an outstanding achievement.'*

Air Marshall Sir Arthur 'Bomber' Harris, whose decision it was to go ahead with such an audacious raid, put it this way:

> *'The gallant adventure penetrating deep into the heart of Germany in daylight and pressed with outstanding determination in the face of bitter and foreseen opposition takes its place among the most courageous operations of the war.'*

Despite the glowing rhetoric, daylight raids at low level were promptly abandoned by Bomber Command. It would forever remain the longest low-level daylight raid ever undertaken during the Second World War.

Five of the seventeen bombs dropped didn't explode, and although heavily damaged, production at the M.A.N. diesel engine factory was only slowed, not stopped. It was back up to full capacity after just six months. So, it could be hailed as an outstanding achievement, certainly, but not an outstanding success.

In recognition of their gallantry, Nettleton was awarded the Victoria Cross, David Penman, and Sherwood the Distinguished Service Order, my father and seven other officers the Distinguished Flying Cross and a clutch of others the Distinguished Flying Medal. My mother always held the view, unsurprisingly, that her Arthur should have had the V.C. but that it went to Nettleton based on rank and the fact that he and his crew got back. Looking at who got what, rank did seem to be a factor, but how can one man's bravery be measured against another's when all faced the same terrifying challenge?

CHAPTER 12

Prisoner 117

Back in Britain, the Augsburg raid was big news both in the press and in cinemas across the land. A Pathé newsreel was screened, complete with patriotic music and an upbeat commentary featuring Nettleton, Penman, and other returning airmen. It inevitably praised the success of the venture at a time when public morale was fragile at best. But for the parents, siblings, wives, and sweethearts of the forty-nine missing men, it was a time of agonising suspense; had they survived, and if so, where were they?

Up in Hexham, Arthur senior, Sarah, his wife, and their two daughters, Beatrice and young Nora, were worried sick but waited in hope, as did Joan Shepherd in Doncaster. The local Hexham Courant newspaper carried a photograph of Arthur with the heading 'Missing after Augsburg raid.' Days passed slowly.

The artist Frank Salisbury had heard the news too and had assumed the worst. On the 28th of April, eleven days after the raid, he picked up a fountain pen and, in elegant handwriting befitting an artist, wrote the following letter to Arthur's parents at 'Viewlands':

Sarum Chase, West Heath Road, Hampstead, NW3.

'Dear Mr & Mrs Garwell,

Mrs Reddell has written to tell me of your terrible trouble. Your dear and gallant son sat for me at Scampton for the picture of The Briefing.

He and Kirke sat for me before they set out for Cologne. On their way back, a Messerschmitt followed and shot off their tail lamps, and they landed at an aerodrome in Norfolk, so they were dead tired when they returned the next morning, but after two hours rest, they were fresh and ready for work. I am having their study mounted and framed and will send it on to you and do hope it will be of some comfort to you.

You know that you have my sincere sympathy - the heart of our Country goes out to you in this sad loss. The dear boys, courageous crusaders, get something of the immensity of space into their natures. Thus, an airman can write to his mother and say, "The universe is so vast and ageless that the life of one man is only justified by the measure of his sacrifices." So, you must be comforted and know that transitory life for all of us is a passing incident and that the soul of your dear and heroic son is in the keeping of the Lord, who knows no limitation of time, and in the briefing room of the eternal. The Master of all great heroes will set their course back on indestructible wings which will outstrip the shadows of our nights.

Yours Sincerely.

Frank O. Salisbury R.A.'

But they had already found out that their son was not, in fact, in the 'briefing room of the eternal' but was very much alive. On the same day that this letter dropped onto the doormat at 'Viewlands,' another one arrived from one of Arthur senior's old schoolmates. It read:

'Dear Arthur,

I have delayed writing to you in the hope of better definite news. This I am delighted to see has come & I sincerely hope your son is safe and uninjured. Kindly accept on behalf of all the old boys our sincere sympathy & we all hope your boy will soon be home again safe and sound. His Mother & Sisters, and of course, his Father must feel very proud of him. Do let me know when he sends you a letter. I have seen Jameson Scott; he had the press cuttings in case I had not seen them, and he wishes to be kindly remembered to you.

Accept all the best from your old pal, Jack Mullen.'

By this time, Frank Salisbury had received the good news too. On the 14th of May, he wrote to Arthur's parents again:

'Dear Mr & Mrs Garwell,

Yesterday I received your wonderful letter containing the news that the Air Ministry had informed you that your fallen son was a prisoner! What a relief to your great anxiety! We shall join with you in keeping him in our prayers. I hope you heard Group Captain Hilmore's tribute in the Sunday Postscript (a BBC radio programme) *to that outstanding historical flight to Augsburg. Those great fellows certainly "left the vivid air signed with their honour." - names that all generations will honour with pride.*

I have sent the sketch of your son off to you today by post & I hope that you will receive it safely. You must remember that it is just a sketch, so you must not expect a finished portrait, but I do hope it will give you pleasure and have a growing historical interest.

With all good wishes

Yours sincerely

Frank O. Salisbury.'

He was first taken to a prison in Munich before being moved to a transit camp called Dulag Luft, near Frankfurt, for interrogation and processing. His first concern was to let his folks know that he was safe, so, on the 20th of April, three days after the crash-landing, he sent a postcard to them. It read:

'Dear Mother and Dad - I trust that you have heard by now that I am ok and hope you didn't worry too much. I am very fit and well and not at all downhearted. You should see me now with a German tunic and a bright red beard going strong! I hope that Beatrice and Nora and yourselves are keeping fit. I am going to make arrangements for some of my pay to be passed on to you. Please write to Joan and let her know I am well. Keep smiling. I'll be back. Love, Arthur.'

It struck exactly the note of reassurance one might expect of a concerned son writing to his worried parents. It also set the tone for all of his later letters home - no self-pity and no sentimentality. I wonder now, all these years later, how he dealt with the shock and trauma of what had just happened. It must have been buried somewhere deep inside. How Fred and Lottie Flux from Southampton, the parents of Bob Flux, would have cherished such a card from their son.

He was soon moved 400 miles east to a newly built prisoner-of-war camp in the German province of Lower Silesia, close to a town called Sagan (now called Zagan and just over the border in Poland). It was the one that would later be made famous by the film 'The Great Escape' - Stalag Luft 3. On the 13th of May, he wrote his first proper letter home:

'Dear Family,

As you see from the address, I have been moved since I wrote to you last. The new place isn't too bad at all, but I haven't settled in properly yet. Time seems to pass fairly quickly and quite pleasantly.

The camp is pretty big – plenty of chaps here, I know – and there's a nice stretch of about half a mile inside the wire for exercise. You know I was supposed to come home on leave the day after I was shot down. Bob couldn't come home with me now anyway; you will be sorry to hear. Frank, my New Zealander, is fit and well. You would no doubt be pleased to hear about Penman, the lucky devil.

About parcels, etc. You will have all the information from the Red Cross, I suppose. I wonder if you could arrange to have some cigarettes sent through the American Tobacco Company. If you send me a personal parcel, please shove in plenty of winter clothing as it will get very cold here around October. There is no limit to the number of letters I am allowed to receive, so get everyone writing. Of course, I am only allowed a very limited number, so I cannot write to many people myself.

Give my regards to all friends – the office staff, Mr & Mrs Potts, all relations – and let them know I am still fighting fit. I am just thinking of studying a few languages – Italian, Spanish, French, and maybe German – so that the next few months or years (I hope not!) will not be wasted. There's a chap in the same room as me – a solicitor – who lived for many years at Wylam. We often talk over the people we know.

I wonder if you would care to have Joan up if she gets a holiday this summer. I am sure she would like to visit you again.

Love to you all.

Arthur.'

Stalag Luft 3 was run by the Luftwaffe specifically for the detention of Allied air force personnel. The guards either were or had been airmen themselves, so they had some natural affinity with the newly arrived inmates and were just as keen to survive the war. The atmosphere was almost gentlemanly, especially early on – it was no concentration camp. The Commandant, Friedrich-Wilhelm von Lindeiner-Wildau, was a highly decorated veteran of the Prussian army and the First World War. He loved his country but despised the Nazi regime and all it stood for. Open-minded and liberal by nature, he was universally respected by his staff and the prisoners in his charge – he had no wish to make their lives more miserable than necessary. He wanted a benign regime. Old school. Firm but fair.

Set in an area of dense dark-green pine forest, the sprawling site was chosen because the sandy soil on which it was built would make tunnelling to escape too difficult – or so it was thought.

Arthur was given the prisoner of war number 117 – Kriegsgefangener 117 in German. His metal identity tag – the one my brother showed me on that cold, wet winter's day in the Dalesman cafe – is now over 80 years old. The inmates of Stalag Luft 3 referred to themselves as 'kriegies' – short for kriegsgefangener – the German word for prisoner of war. They called the guards 'goons'. The Germans, of course, were completely unaware of the comical connotation this nickname had for the men in their charge.

He was initially housed in the East Compound, the first to be built. It contained fifteen long, single-story wooden huts, each housing some 120 prisoners. The huts were divided into small rooms for sleeping, typically measuring just 10 feet by 12 feet. Each one of these rooms slept 6 to 8 men in bunk beds. There was one toilet per hut for use at night, a communal kitchen, and a washroom. It was cramped, to say the least.

All letters sent from the camp were first read by German examiners - mainly young women - and, if thought necessary, censored. They were written in pencil on a single sheet of airmail paper which was then folded and closed with a paper tab. The examiner, once satisfied that the contents were not a security risk, stuck on a label showing their identity number and stamped on the front 'Gepruft' - the German word for checked. All mail, both incoming and outgoing, was sent via Geneva in neutral Switzerland. Very few of Arthur's letters required any censorship. On the 29th of May, he wrote:

> 'Dear Family - I trust that you have received some of my letters by now. This is communication number five. It is six weeks today since I was shot down. I am getting fairly well accustomed to the ife - if you can call it such. This place is a long way from England, and the weather is much hotter in summer - and a lot colder in winter, I should imagine. I trust that you have some warm clothing and bags of cigarettes on the way. I left my tunic behind, and it was burned.

> *I have a bit of garden here and am trying to grow a few things - radishes, lettuce, turnips, spinach, etc. We even hope to have a few tomatoes.'*

It may seem surprising that gardening was possible in a prisoner of war camp, but allowing such activities helped to keep boredom at bay and served to supplement the meagre food rations. Seeds for planting came from the Red Cross or from German guards who would exchange them for whatever items the kriegies had to offer – mainly cigarettes.

He continued:

> *'I hope that everyone is fit and well, including my little godson. I can't, of course, write to everyone I would like, so I hope you will let them know I am well. I have met a chap here who is a Customs Officer, and he has told me a lot about the job. It sounds very interesting. Have you heard from the bank yet? I wrote to them five weeks ago. Keep writing to me. Cheerio. Love to you all. Arthur.'*

He'd not long arrived but was already thinking about what his career might be when the war finished.

May soon gave way to June, but there was no post from home yet. On the 18th of June, he wrote:

> *'Dear Family,*
>
> *Two months over now, and things are still jogging along much the same. I have delayed writing to you this month in the hope that I might hear from you, but so far, nothing has turned up. I trust that by now, you have managed to get some tobacco parcels on the way. I hope too that you have made contact with someone in America who can send me some food. I should also like my tunic, as I lost my battledress when the aircraft burned.*

Things seem to be getting along quite nicely at home. We get new people in here pretty often and collect scraps of news. We have a paper issued to us called the 'Camp' which is pretty useful for one thing which you can no doubt guess. (I couldn't, but the next sentence served as an explanation). *I see in it that Sunderland have reached the final of the League Cup. Pretty good going.* (His dad was a lifelong Sunderland supporter).

Cooking and gardening seem to take up most of my time. We are trying to grow some tomatoes, but the soil is not very good. Cooking I find most interesting. We managed to concoct some of the most amazing recipes, which we appreciate here, but I doubt if we would have done so three months ago. Well, I haven't heard from you yet, but I trust you are all keeping fit and very well. Give my love to Nora and Bee.

Cheerio. Arthur.'

Failures and successes in the growing of tomatoes became a frequent topic in later letters – a far cry from failures and successes in bombing raids.

Four days later and there was still no news from home. Worried, he wrote:

'Dear Mum & Dad,

This is my seventh letter to you. I hope you have received the others O.K. I haven't heard from you yet but no doubt something will turn up in time. It's rather worrying, though, not knowing if you have heard that I am safe or not.'

Then on the 30th of June:

'Dear Family - this is my eighth letter to you, and so far, I have had nothing from you. Before I go any further, I have a request. Could

you please send me a medical comforts parcel? You are allowed to send one when I was shot down and so many after that. I don't know the number, but the Red Cross will tell you. Porridge, milk, etc., would be very welcome. I wrote a card to Nora yesterday. You will probably get it along with this letter.

Life here goes along fairly smoothly. I find myself reverting to my old hobby of gardening, only this time it is not quite as hectic as it used to be. I have a fine selection of tomatoes which are doing pretty nicely. The weather is sometimes most unhelpful, and the sun burns everything off. I often wonder how things are going on the right side of the North Sea these days. Is the old car still going strong, or have you laid it up? I hope not. I shall write to everyone in turn if I am here long enough.'

With his old crewmate and friend still in mind, he then wrote:

'I wonder if you have heard anything from Mrs Flux. If so, you might send the address as I ought to write to her about Bob. He was not wounded at all but was killed instantly when we landed. He was very brave throughout the trip and helped me a lot, as he always did.'

He wanted Bob's parents to at least know that their son hadn't suffered in his final moments.

'Well, I hope I shall hear from England before I write to you again. Cheerio. Love to all. Arthur.'

Shortly after this, he did hear from England, and on the 9th of July, he was relieved to write:

'Dear Family,

I was delighted to receive thirteen letters from you yesterday. Apart from one from the bank which reached me a week ago, these are the first I have had. I received seven from Joan, four from you, one from Beatrice, and one from Mr Potts. I am so glad to hear that you are all well and that you heard in good time. It must have been a big worry for you though I had hoped you would guess from reports that I had made it O.K.'

Then it was quickly down to practical matters:

'There are a few points I must deal with now, first clothes. I shall write to have things released as soon as I have a spare card. I hardly think it is worth sending my tunic now anyway. Pen, wallet, writing case, and caps were all in my room and ought to be on the list unless someone has pinched them. I should write to the adjutant of my station. Now about the bank. I want you to use ten pounds per month of that money yourselves as you need it. Don't forget that tax is paid at source. Thanks for fixing savings.

I was sorry to hear that Beatrice failed half of her exam (she was training to be a nurse). *I knew she would manage practical O.K. Still, she ought to make it easily next time. It's a pity I missed that cake which you made, Mother, but I shall make up for it when I get back. I have just made a very excellent walnut cake – good by our standards at least!'*

Food was never far from the prisoners' thoughts: camp rations alone were not enough to fill stomachs to anything like satisfaction, so Red Cross parcels were vital to maintain camp morale and keep hunger at bay. They were not wasted:

'Time passes fairly quickly here. The days drift by, and so long as our Red Cross food parcels arrive, everyone seems to be reasonably happy. Speaking of food, I must tell you about a meal we had yesterday. It was to celebrate a 21st birthday and also a wedding anniversary. We had saved up for a week and managed to turn out five courses. We

started off with fishcakes, then had a large plate of bacon, sausage, chips, tomatoes, and a German dish called noodles which is something like macaroni. This was followed by a sweet, rather like Christmas cake with sauce, then a savoury, then coffee and cake. The cake was made by me. It was a chocolate fruit cake, but I regret to state that it did not quite reach the standard one would expect from the son of an expert. It was soggy with a texture like wet concrete, but my objective was achieved, for it filled and floored us to a man and everyone was happy, though a little sick.'

And still on the subject of food:

'I am so glad you are having Joan up in August and that you are teaching her to cook. She needs a bit of tuition! Pouring out poached eggs!! The holiday ought to do her a lot of good. This war has been most unkind to her.'

It was hardly surprising that Joan couldn't cook, having lost her mother when she was just nine years old. Arthur's mother was determined to fix this shortcoming if Joan was to be the future wife of her only son.

The letters from home had contained some news that he referred to next:

'Your news of a D.F.C. was the first I had heard. Did my crew get anything? Keeps the old Garwell flag flying anyway. The little beggars I used to teach have had some good out of me after all.

Please don't worry about me. I am doing fine here. I trust that Nora is well and has written to me.

Cheerio.

Your loving son.

Arthur.

P.S. Don't write to Geneva. My address is underlined. D.F.C. comes first, by the way!!'

His award of the Distinguished Flying Cross had been announced in the London Gazette on the 5th of June (where all military awards were listed), and the news had spread quickly. Letters of congratulations began to arrive at 'Viewlands,' like this one from the district manager of the Pearl Assurance Company Limited, Arthur senior's employer, addressed to his wife:

'Dear Mrs Garwell,

The news that Arthur is safe and well and that he has been awarded the D.F.C. is great. I am delighted! Of course, the award is of small importance as compared with his safety & well-being, but even so, it is a great honour to be awarded the D.F.M. & D.F.C. Mr Garwell & yourself must be very proud of your brave son - and you have every right to be so.

Kind Regards. Sincerely yours. Lionel Gardner.'

And this from the former headmaster of his old junior school at nearby Acomb:

'Dear Arthur,

We have just heard on the one o'clock news of the further honour gained by Arthur junior for the Augsburg raid, and we hasten to congratulate him through you.

We shared your anxiety through those anxious days following the exploit and were delighted when we saw in the newspapers that he was safe. It is an honour of the highest magnitude to have taken part in such a magnificent venture, and you must feel very proud. For my part, too, I share your pride. Beyond his personal courage (he always was as game as a pebble), he is, without doubt, a most skilful pilot; what we owe to the likes of him! Do remember me to him when you write to him and wish him all the best from me. And ask him if he would drop me a card sometime. I should appreciate it so much. Further, would you send his address? I hope he will not have too bad a time in Germany and soon be restored safely to you.

Kindest regards from us both to Mrs Garwell, Beatrice, Norah, and yourself.

Yours Sincerely. J Elliott.

P.S. Acomb had the goods after all! Bravo!!!'

The local vicar of St. John Lee church was equally excited by the news and wrote:

'*Dear Mr and Mrs Garwell,*

When I heard the news of the honour that Arthur had won on the radio today, I went down to announce it to the children. They were very proud to know that an old scholar of Acomb School had been awarded the D.F.C. and asked me to convey to you both their delight and to wish that Arthur will soon return safely to you. Incidentally, they were released from school earlier to mark the occasion.

My wife and I wish to add our good wishes to you and know that you must be very proud of your gallant son. We, like the children, hope that you will soon have him back home.

Yours sincerely,

W.H.S. Wood.'

Even the branch manager of the family's bank, the National Provincial, put pen to paper - this being in the days, long since passed, of old-fashioned banking when the personal touch mattered:

'Dear Mr Garwell,

Just a few lines to say how pleased we all are to know that Arthur has been further honoured by H.M. The King. Hearty congratulations to him and to you! And may you soon have him home again in normal life.'

He might have been very much the local hero in Hexham and the surrounding area, but his own concerns were altogether more pragmatic: food, clothing, boredom, the future, and the possibility of escape. And cigarettes.

Brew time at Stalag Luft 3: Ginger Garwell with fellow prisoner Flying Officer Davidson. The pine trees that surrounded the camp can be seen in the background.

CHAPTER 13

Summer Heat and Thoughts of Love

Four months in, and letters from home were now arriving regularly. On August 7th, he wrote:

'Dear Family, I have just received your letter this evening dated 15/7. I am glad to hear that you are all hard at work in the garden. I wouldn't mind betting you mess the thing up, though.'

He'd heard that Joan was spending her summer holiday with his family at 'Viewlands' and couldn't resist some more leg-pulling. There was a lot of that in the camp.

'You'd better watch Joan too. She's no gardener, and as for cooking – God, you'll need some bottles of those laxative things you take. Don't tell her I said that, whatever you do.'

Thinking of his post-war future, he then wrote:

'I am glad that you have heard from the Customs people and that everything is O.K. for after the war. There is a Customs officer here whom I know pretty well. He reckons it's the finest job in the world.'

He would have other ideas about a career later in his captivity - there was a lot of time to think and plan.

Although letters were getting through, parcels were a different matter:

'It's a good thing you have got that parcel off. I hope it reaches me before Christmas. I haven't received any cigarettes yet, but when they do come, there ought to be a pretty steady flow, judging from the number of people who seem to have sent me some. When they do come, I shall smoke and smoke till I've put up a colossal smoke screen then − under cover of it − walk over the wire, eh!'

The business of escaping would, in time, become what Stalag Luft 3 was famous for. He might only have been joking at this stage of his captivity, but that was to change soon enough.

His next words were, of necessity, cryptic:

'I understand from Bee that Ron has moved. I have a feeling that his firm ought to be busy very shortly.'

Captain Ronald E. G. Curtis, Beatrice's boyfriend, was attached to the 535 Company Guards Armoured Division of what was to become the British Liberation Army. It would, though, be another two years before his 'firm' was busy in the way that Arthur implied.

He continued:

'I haven't heard from any relatives or friends yet except for the letter from Bee and one from Mr Potts. I have, however, been very fortunate in receiving twelve from Joan. My letters do not seem to be reaching you as quickly as they might. This is the eleventh I have written to you.'

The Summer of 1942 was, in that part of central Europe at least, searingly hot. In his next letter home, dated September 5th, he wrote:

'Dear Family, I received your letter of August 4th some days ago. I have also heard from Beatrice, and today I received another letter

from Joan. Mail seems to come through here very quickly - I have had most of mine in three weeks. I gather from your letter that the summer In England has not been as fine as it might have been. I have never known such heat as we have had here. The temperature in the sun seems to hover between 140 and 150 every day. It gets so hot in the evening that I often sleep till about 3 am on top of the bed! I have no doubt we shall get a spot of the cold stuff in a month or two, but I hope that the parcel you sent me will have arrived to save the situation. I have not received any cigarettes yet, but they ought to be here soon.

The garden here has been a bit of a failure. The heat combined with the poor soil - which is pure sand - made failure pretty certain anyway. We hope to get about 30 tomatoes plus a few cabbages and maybe a potato or two. Your tales of mushrooms, tomatoes, peas, etc., I find very impressive. However, I shall certainly make up the leeway when I get home.'

The next paragraph illustrates the slightly bizarre lengths that kriegies would go to in their attempts to stem the day-in, day-out, boredom of camp life:

'Today we are having an ersatz Race Meeting. The horses move by dice, but apart from that, everything else is genuine - the bookmakers, tipsters, fortune tellers, tote, band, and even the Salvation Army, which came along to preach the evils of gambling!!'

Putting on entertainment like this and going to great lengths to make it realistic became a big part of camp life. In time the kriegies built their own theatre, made their own costumes, and put on the latest shows from London's West End. Some went on to have lifelong careers in acting after the war - there was an abundance of talent cooped up in those long, low, wooden huts surrounded by barbed wire and guard towers.

Frivolous diversions were all well and good, but Arthur's thoughts were never far away from the girl he'd left behind. Referring again to Joan's summer holiday at 'Viewlands,' he wrote:

'I gather from Joan's letter that she seems to be having a very fine time with you. I am so glad.

I have a feeling that someone will have to buy an engagement ring for me in the near future unless the boys come over to take us back very soon.'

Being just twenty-two years old and in love made camp life so much more bearable; a feeling of optimism pervaded his letters home.

It wasn't just Arthur either - in the next letter home, he wrote:

'I was delighted to hear of Bee's engagement. I am very short of mail, so please convey my congratulations to Bee. Could you also arrange to buy them a suitable present and let me know the cost? I hope that you have received my letter in which I asked you about Joan and myself. My congratulations are also due to you two on your Silver Wedding Anniversary. You seem to have had a very fine party. It was very nice of the staff to have that little ceremony. What about buying yourselves a little present? You might shake up the bank & find out the state of my account for me. They have only sent me one statement in seven months.'

Not all news from home was good news:

'I was very sorry to hear that poor old Granda had passed on but glad that he did not have any prolonged illness. He was a big age. I

wish I could have been back to see him again. He would be buried at Mickley, I suppose. That leaves only my grandmother of the old brigade. Do you ever see her these days? I often wonder if her hair is still the same bright red.'

Letters were getting through regularly, but there had been no parcels from home in seven months of captivity. Then, finally, one arrived, and it was exactly what he needed as colder weather approached:

'I received my first clothing parcel on November 11th. Many thanks. It was an excellent effort, and nothing was missing. Please thank all who contributed. Suggestions for next parcel: Hair oil, bath towel, boot polish, gym shoes, sports shirt, shorts.'

There was a lot of sports activity at Stalag Luft 3; it played a vital role in maintaining the mental and physical well-being of the men. Cricket and football dominated, especially among the British contingent - and Ginger Garwell was a decent fast bowler. Inter-hut cricket teams were named after English counties, and competition was fierce. Pride was at stake. Likewise, with football - most of the men got to play at least one game a week, and the pitch was in frequent use between matches. Officers versus orderlies were one of the top fixtures, attracting large crowds and summoning up the atmosphere of a cup-tie back home. In a later letter, he wrote:

'We have a fine soccer Association running now. I am playing for Arsenal in the first league. Have won both our matches 3-0 & 6-0.'

Volleyball, boxing, gymnastics, tennis, and table tennis were also popular. Failing this, there was always the option of walking around the long perimeter fence to dissipate pent-up energy -

and there was no shortage of that.

Sport, food, and women - or the lack of them - might have occupied the thoughts of most kriegies, but there was something almost equally important - cigarettes:

'I have also received one parcel of 500 fags from my Group Captain. I received a letter the other day from a Mrs Lees, 5 South Park, Hexham, saying that the Inner Wheel Club or something had held whist drives, etc. & was sending me a Christmas parcel. Will you please thank Mrs Lees from me & explain the shortage of letters, etc.'

And then followed an almost throwaway sentence that would, in time, prove to be life-changing:

'By the way, I managed to rake up a letter and write to Joan's father about engagement, so that ought to be O.K.'

It seems old-fashioned now, asking a father's permission for the hand of his daughter in marriage, but it would have been poor form not to do so back then. Albert Shepherd agreed, of course. Why wouldn't he?

'Well, that seems to be all. Don't worry about me. I am very fit & well & have plenty of clothes for the winter. Give my love to Cousin Ruth & Nora. Oh yes, I nearly forgot Christmas. I'm sorry I can't send a card. I do wish you all a very good time. Let's hope we are all together for the next one. Love, Arthur.'

As the end of the year approached and war raged on outside the camp, there was time to write one more letter home:

'Dec 10th, 1942

Dear Family - Many thanks for your letters of Nov 4th and 13th. I am happy to know that you are all well. As for me, I am very fit.

I have only once been to the doctor since I came here, and that was to have a swab taken because one of my roommates had diphtheria. Fortunately, he recovered quickly, and no one else caught it. In the summer, we all had very mild doses of something like dysentery, but that was due to the heat and tinned food. Of course, I don't put on much weight! But you can see that there is no reason to worry about me.'

The POWs in Stalag Luft 3 were generally well looked after. Most remained in surprisingly good physical health in spite of the crowding, inadequate sanitary facilities, and limited medical supplies. In the absence of plumbing, both indoor and outdoor latrines contributed to the sanitation problem, especially in summer. Washing facilities were severely limited. For those unlucky enough to fall seriously ill, each compound in the camp had its own sick quarters staffed by orderlies and doctors drawn from the prison population. They were stocked with medical supplies sent, whenever possible, by the Red Cross.

Arthur was lucky to be fit and healthy - enough to turn his hand to a spot of manual labour:

'At the moment, I am actually doing a bit of work on a theatre we are building. I mix cement and carry bricks and dig a bit of sand now and then.'

The way the Luftwaffe ran the camp was, maybe surprisingly given what was happening elsewhere, relatively humane. Allowing prisoners to be engaged in such an enterprise kept them occupied and, perhaps they thought, less desperate to escape. In that, of course, they were mistaken - as time would tell.

Something else that could constructively fill the time was reading, especially relating to any subject that might be useful in the future. Arthur had intended to study a number of different languages when first arriving at the camp, but that hadn't quite worked out:

'As far as study is concerned, I have done very little except learn a spot of German. Your books, by the way, have not turned up yet.'

Swiftly changing the subject to the painting by Frank Salisbury that he and Kirke had sat for at RAF Scampton, he then writes:

'I gather from your letter that the Briefing picture has been receiving a lot of publicity lately. The two people you asked about are Wing Commander Boyle and Squadron Leader Forsyth.

Will you please tell Ted Glenwright how sorry I am to hear about Campbell. If he is over here, I don't think he will come to this camp, so I cannot find out anything about him.

About my kit. You will have to write for it. The raincoat was probably down in one of the offices on the aerodrome. Don't worry about it. There should be a wallet with probably £5 in it - I'm not sure of the amount. My side cap, I think, was with me in the aeroplane and was probably burned. I don't remember.'

Finally, some quick-fire responses to news from home:

'I was very surprised to hear of the death of Reverend Wood. (The vicar who'd written to congratulate Arthur's parents a few months earlier) *He got away quickly. Stagshaw won't be the same without Mr Morrow. Please give him my regards when next you see him. I am looking forward very much to visiting the beautiful chapel again. I am very glad Uncle Tommy looks like getting his farm soon. Tell him to breed game so that the poachers of the family can have a spot of legitimate fun for a change! As for Ron's music, please tell*

him not to send it. I have a half share in an accordion, but every time I pick it up, I am liable to have my brains dashed out with a log or something by angry roommates!

Please give my congratulations to Nora on her performance in exams. She looks like she is turning out pretty good. Had a cigarette parcel from Joan today. Cheerio. Best love to you all. Arthur.'

And that was it. Christmas came and went, and 1942 drew to a close. Freezing winter snowfall swirled around the pine trees and settled on the wooden roofs of the huts as the inmates of Stalag Luft 3 struggled to keep warm. He'd been in captivity for seven months.

Photo sent to Joan in October 1942.
L-R Jessop, Ramsay, Willis-Richards, Garwell.

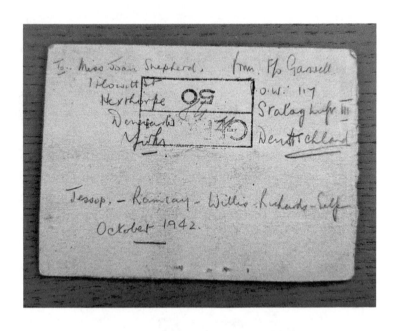

To Miss Joan Shepherd,   from P/o Gansell
     Flowitt   O.W. 117
   Nexthorpe   [50]   Stalaglufr III
   Denmark   Deutschland
   Yorks

Jessop, — Ramsay — Willis. Richards–Self

   October 1942.

CHAPTER 14

Spring 1943

Briggs Motor Bodies - the name sticks in my memory from childhood. It was an American company from Detroit, which, as the name suggests, made motor car parts, mainly for the Ford Motor Company - not that I knew that back then. To me, it was where my mum went to work during the war, and they made aeroplane parts.

It seems that it all came about by chance; a huge engineering metal press had been built in Scotland and was on its way by rail to a customer in France when war broke out. To stop it from falling into enemy hands, the press was shunted into a railway siding in Doncaster and all but forgotten. Meanwhile, Briggs Motor Bodies, which was by now making parts for Ford at Dagenham in Essex, had decided to open a factory in the north to try and avoid the heavy German bombing in and around London. They chose the industrial town of Doncaster, which is where they chanced upon exactly what they needed - a very large, brand new engineering press languishing, unloved, in a railway goods yard. The machine was moved to a former railway wagon works at Carr Hill, and production commenced, but not of motor cars.

As the war got underway, manufacturing companies of all shapes and sizes were switching production to make desperately needed parts to support the war effort, and Briggs Motor Bodies was no exception. They were assigned to manufacture engine cowlings and manifolds for the newly developed de Havilland Mosquito, the fastest multi-use warplane the world had seen up to then. It was a super-lightweight aircraft with a fuselage constructed of birch plywood and wings covered in doped cotton fabric upon which were mounted two huge Rolls Royce Merlin engines. Nicknamed the 'Wooden Wonder,' it had to be fast, or it would have been shot to pieces in an instant.

Included in the 223 companies subcontracted to make parts for the Mosquito were furniture factories, cabinetmakers, luxury auto coachbuilders, and, almost incredibly, piano makers. The list included names that it's now hard to imagine being associated with warfare: Electrolux, Addis Brushes, Decca Records, Parker-Knoll, Vauxhall, and even the bicycle manufacturer Claud Butler. But the business of Briggs Motor Bodies was metal, not wood, and the factory in which its products were made echoed with the ear-splitting crash and thump of giant presses. It was a far cry from the hush of Dr Wallis's dental practice, where young Joan Shepherd had previously been employed.

'I understand that you have had Joan up for a short holiday. I am very sorry that she has had to leave her job. I am afraid the new one will not be so pleasant.'

He was right - the factory floor was not a happy place for a sensitive girl with a southern accent and a nervous disposition. The women that worked there - for most of the manual labour during the war was carried out by women - were a tough lot from a tough working-class town, and Joan didn't fit in. She'd been taunted for her accent at school, but this was much worse. The bullying was relentless, so much so that her workshop foreman couldn't ignore it, and she was finally moved to a position in the administration office. It was a much better fit.

Arthur was about to move too. On March 29th, he wrote to his family:

> *'We are expecting to move to a new camp early next week. It is quite near to this place and should be a little more comfortable. It will be a very pleasant change anyway. The address I expect will be the same.'*

The move was from the East Compound to a newly built North Compound. With the relentless influx of new arrivals, expansion of the camp was essential, and the new compound, built to house RAF airmen, added another 15 single-storey wooden huts to increase its capacity. It would, in time, become famous as the launch pad of the 'Great Escape.' But more of that later.

Far away from the ordered isolation of Stalag Luft 3, in Stalingrad, Russia, some 1,500 miles to the east, the biggest and bloodiest battle of the war had just ended. The city lay in ruins. After five months of relentless battle, the German 6th Army had finally surrendered to the Russians. For the first time since the outbreak of war in 1939, the Nazi government announced a defeat on state radio. The tide was turning – and news of it soon circulated around the camp.

The depths of human suffering endured by both sides is hard to imagine. It had started with a Luftwaffe bombing offensive that unleashed more destruction on Stalingrad than London had suffered in the Blitz. The Russian Red Army was pushed back through the city to the banks of the Volga River and all but overrun by the Nazi onslaught. It is said that Stalin would not allow the evacuation of the city's inhabitants because he decided his troops were more likely to fight to the last man with a civilian population to protect. Vicious street-by-street combat saw the

German forces all but take the city until the Russians mounted a last-ditch counter-offensive, attacking the weaker flanks of the 6th Army and eventually surrounding it. It was by then the middle of winter. Cut off from supplies of ammunition and food, except for the severely limited amount the Luftwaffe could drop from the air, the only hope of survival was to try and break out of the Red Army's stranglehold and link up with German forces on the other side of the blockade. Hitler, though, would not allow such a humiliating capitulation and demanded they fight to the death. Freezing and starving, with over 40,000 sick and wounded men and no medical supplies with which to treat them, they eventually gave in and, unit by unit surrendered. By the time it ended, some two million soldiers and civilians were dead, wounded, or missing, over half of them Russian.

As the new North compound of Stalag Luft 3 began to fill with Allied airmen, over 90,000 German troops, many in a pitiful state, were being taken captive in Russia. Most of them ended up in Russian labour camps where they died of their wounds, the cold, disease, or mistreatment. Only some 5,000 of them ever saw their homeland again.

My father's letters home was in stark contrast to such horrors. Take this postcard written to his mother just before the move to the new compound:

'Dear Mother,

Many thanks for your letter of Nov 24th, which has only just reached me this evening. Our mail has been coming through pretty badly recently. I thank you for your Christmas wishes. I had a pretty good time but not like home, as you will appreciate. You ask how I spend my time. It is difficult to say, but the days seem to drift by pretty *quickly. I have my books now, of course, and do a fair amount of study but find it difficult to concentrate. I am glad to hear that Nora is getting on so well. Have you any snaps you could send me sometime? I have two which I will send in my next letter. Heard from Joan yesterday. She seems to be getting along pretty well.*

Hoping to see you soon.

Your loving son,

Arthur.'

Days could never *'drift by'* in a Russian labour camp. That's not to suggest that it was an easy existence for the airmen cooped up in Stalag Luft 3, but it was more than bearable. Catching up with news from home helped to keep it that way:

'April 24th, 1943

Dear Family,

After a longish period without much mail, I had four letters from you on the 21st. I was very pleased to hear that everything is going well at 'Viewlands.' I was surprised to find that Bee had changed hospitals. She will no doubt be happier nearer home and relatives, and the extra salary is a good thing. How is Ron these days? I never hear from him.

You will soon know if Nora has managed to pass her exam. I hope she has. I am sorry Norman Ridley has been unlucky. My memory is not so good where names are concerned, I'm afraid, and it took me some time to work out who he is. I haven't come across him here.

By the way, have you received payment from the bank yet for that engagement ring? I wrote to them some time ago, but the letter may not have got through as there was a ban on letters to banks.

Will you please give my thanks to Aunt Betty and Uncle Tommy for the Christmas present? I had a letter from Cousin Ruth in which she said they were expecting to move soon. I have just written off a card to Miss Dodd as requested. I hope that it arrives on time. I thought that I was safe from such things here, but apparently, I was wrong!

We are now in our new camp. It is a bit more pleasant than the last one. The weather has been very good recently – some days being about as hot as England in August. I'd sooner have England in August, though.

My uniform and December parcels haven't arrived yet, but I am expecting them any day. Many thanks for sending off extra cigarettes.

My love to you all.

Arthur.'

Back in Arthur's hometown, preparations were underway for the Hexham and District 'Wings for Victory Week' with the aim of raising £250,000 towards the war effort. I have the official programme. It starts with this message from the Speaker of the House of Commons, Colonel the Right Hon. Douglas Clifton Brown:

"I urge everyone to invest more savings this time. Remember that without the money provided by you, our Sailors, Soldiers, and Airmen cannot win the victory that we all desire, and without which England and all that Great Britain and the Empire stands for cannot survive. The more we save now and lend to the country, the quicker the victorious end will come."

A message from the Chairmen of the Hexham Urban & Rural District Council is even more insistent:

'Three and three-quarter years of war, and still you are asked to save. WHY?

Ships, guns, shells, torpedoes, and aeroplanes have been produced in ever-increasing numbers, and still, you are asked to save. WHY?

Thousands of millions of pounds have been saved, and still, you are asked to save. WHY?

Because the job is not yet finished. Because the sternest part of the struggle is yet to come. Because nothing short of complete and unequivocal victory can give us the security with which to rebuild our national life. Because nothing short of that security can make rebuilding anything but a grim preparation for a further struggle with those that seek to destroy all that we value in life.

You have heard the ominous words scores of times "From all these operations, fifteen - eighteen - thirty of our bombers are missing." £600,000 - £700,000 - £1,200,000 gone in a night. Not all your saving can replace the gallant crews, but only by continued saving can the bombers be replaced, ready for the equally gallant crews who stand ready to take the places of those who have gone on ahead. Shall they wait impatiently because the bombers are not forthcoming?

"WINGS FOR VICTORY," answers Hexham - that we may give Wings TO Victory.'

The programme goes on to list the week's events, including a grand parade of all the services, various lectures by notable local dignitaries, music on the Abbey grounds, whist drives, a children's pet night, and a demonstration by Miss Taylor at 7 pm. Somewhat curiously, it doesn't say exactly what Miss Taylor was going to demonstrate.

As the war raged on, Arthur's letters spoke about the ordinary things of home and prison life, but there was something going on in the new camp that was truly extraordinary.

Back row: Garwell, Cordwell, Hughes, Willis-Richards.
Front row: Jessop, Forfar, Davidson, Ramsay.

Cordwell and Garwell. Others unnamed. Photo taken May 1943.

Another photo from May 1943.
Standing: Cordwell, Garwell, Davidson, Hamilton, Jessop,
Van Toen, Michell. Seated: Ramsay, Hughes, Samson, Meara.

CHAPTER 15

The X Factor

Squadron Leader Roger Bushell arrived at Stalag Luft 3 in the Autumn of 1942. He already had form. Originally from South Africa, born to English parents, he studied law at Cambridge, excelled at sport, especially skiing, and joined the RAF in 1932. A born leader with a formidable intellect, he rose through the ranks rapidly and, soon after the outbreak of war, was given command of a fighter squadron. It was to be short-lived. In May 1940, while engaging the enemy in the skies above Dunkirk, his Spitfire was shot down, crash-landing in German-occupied France, where he was captured and taken prisoner.

Arriving at a Dulag Luft transit camp, he was soon made second-in-command of its already established escape committee and set about organising the digging of a tunnel. It took months. In the end, he escaped alone and above ground, having hidden in a hut in the camp's exercise field for six hours until night fell with the hut's only occupant - a goat - for company. With forged papers, civilian clothes, and his fluent command of the German language, he got as far as the Swiss border - but no further.

Back in captivity, Bushell pulled off a second audacious escape - this time from a train in transit between camps. He succeeded in cutting a hole in the wooden floor of the cattle car with a makeshift saw, then dropped through to the track below while the train was still moving. Accompanied by a Czech fighter pilot, he travelled by normal passenger train to Prague in Czechoslovakia, where the two of them went into hiding until the Gestapo flushed them out. After a gruelling interrogation, Bushell was handed over to the Luftwaffe, which is how he ended up in Stalag Luft 3. His experience left him with a deep hatred, not of the German people – he had spent time there before the war and admired their culture – but of the brutal Nazi regime and its fanatical ethos.

Bushell's reputation as a hardened escape artist, but with the sharp brain of a lawyer, went before him. He was soon put in charge of the Stalag Luft 3 Escape Committee and given the codename 'Big X.'

Like my father, he moved to the newly built North Compound in the Spring of 1943 and immediately began planning what would become the most famous – and infamous – mass prison breakout of the Second World War – 'The Great Escape.'

The idea was to dig not one but three separate tunnels through the sandy soil beneath the huts. They would be codenamed 'Tom,' 'Dick,' and 'Harry.' Each would emerge in the pine trees on the other side of the perimeter fence allowing over 200 men to escape in one attempt. If one tunnel was discovered, there would still be two more chances of success. Work on the project started immediately. It took a year to complete.

Tunnelling in the sandy soil of the camp presented a massive challenge. For one thing, any excavations would quickly collapse unless shored up with timber which, inevitably, was in short supply. It had to be scavenged from wherever it could be found in the camp without the guards noticing. Bed boards were a favourite source. Another of my mother's oft-repeated stories involved one of my father's camp roommates, a young airman from Reading by the name of Reginald Van Toen. She told me that whenever a certain record was played - the frantic finale of 'The Dance of the Hours' by Ponchielli - Van Toen would smash up his bed in an outburst of pent-up frustration. Apparently, the task of rebuilding it helped alleviate his boredom. It's easy to surmise that each time the bed was put back together, there was one less board under the mattress.

The Luftwaffe guards were constantly alert to the possibility of escape attempts, so the tunnel entrances had to be very carefully concealed; it called for great skill and ingenuity. The entrance to 'Tom' was cut into the thick concrete floor in a dark corner of Hut 123. The opening for 'Dick' was created beneath a water-filled sump in the washhouse of Hut 122. The water had to be drained, then refilled to allow access to the tunnel shaft, a process that needed repeating to let the tunnellers back out. The entrance for 'Harry' was hidden beneath a tiled floor that covered the concrete base of a stove in Hut 104. To gain access, the stove had to be lifted off the base, even if still alight, so that the heavy concrete trapdoor could be removed. It took two men to do it. Joints around the closed trap doors were concealed with a mixture of cement dust and soap, making them all but invisible. Tunnel entrances could be opened, closed, and concealed in a matter of seconds. They had to be - guards could appear at any moment, night, or day.

The wooden huts were built on support pillars of brick or concrete, allowing enough space for guards to crawl underneath to check for any irregular activity. These pillars had to be hollowed out to hide the vertical tunnel shafts before they disappeared below ground. The shafts needed to be deep so that the constant activity of digging would not be picked up by the numerous microphones placed in the soil at strategic intervals by the ever-suspicious Germans. The tunnellers dug nine metres straight down before they were deep enough to start the horizontal shafts. The longest tunnel, 'Harry,' had to stretch for 100 metres to comfortably clear the camp's boundary fence. Digging while laid prostrate in a 60 centimetres square shaft with nine metres of sand bearing its full weight on homemade wooden shuttering was not for the faint-hearted.

As the tunnels grew in length, the problem of how to get men to the face had to be solved - it took the creation of a miniature railway to do it. Wooden rails were crafted and laid, and a system of wheeled trolleys pulled by ropes was designed and made. Fresh air was essential, or the diggers would suffocate in the hot, humid conditions deep underground. It was got to them via a ventilation duct made out of empty powdered milk tins laid end to end - they were the ideal size and readily available. Air was pumped through using large homemade bellows.

Then there was the problem of how to dispose of the excavated sand - tons of it - without being spotted by the lookout guards perched high up in the wooden guard towers (which the kriegies called 'goonboxes') or those on foot patrol. It was a different colour to the topsoil and not easy to hide, so many devious methods had to be devised. Pouches made from towels or underpants were hidden inside prisoners' trousers so that the sand could be discreetly scattered as they walked - or rather waddled - around the camp. Filled pouches were heavy, and walking with them awkward, which is why the soil disposal men got to be nicknamed 'penguins.' Some of the sand was surreptitiously deposited in the vegetable gardens as two prisoners pretended to be casually chatting. Arthur Garwell, as his letters show, was a keen gardener. He knew exactly what was going on.

Everyone was sworn to complete secrecy, with no questions to be asked about anything even slightly unusual. 'Big X' made sure of it; *"If you see me walking around with a tree trunk sticking out of my arse, don't ask any questions because it'll be for a damned good reason."*

I remember as a child, my mother telling me of a line in one of my father's wartime letters to her about making use of a secret meeting place from their courting days - only they could know that it was a disused railway tunnel. She guessed what he was hinting at.

The guards knew something was going on; they just didn't know what. It was a constant game of cat and mouse - like a Tom & Jerry cartoon but with higher stakes. There were frequent, unannounced searches of the huts by specialist teams of unarmed guards that the kriegies referred to as 'ferrets' - their sole purpose was to ferret out illegal activities and thwart escape attempts. Ever suspicious, they took great pride in being good at their work. The most tenacious, incorruptible, and feared ferret of all earned the nickname 'Rubberneck.'

As if this highly complex and difficult tunnelling exercise was not enough to be going on with, in the early summer of 1943 'Big X' set about masterminding and executing an almost equally audacious breakout attempt; one that would see my father and twenty-five others simply walk out of the camp and disappear into the pine forest.

CHAPTER 16

The Delousing Party

One damp, cold November day in the year 2020 (when the world was busy fighting a war against an invisible virus), a handwritten envelope dropped through our letterbox and landed on the doormat with a soft thud. Intrigued, I opened it and took out four typed sheets of A4 paper. The first sheet read:

> 'The information contained in this report is to be treated as <u>SECRET</u>.'

> Account of escape of Wing Commander Roland Robert Stanford-Tuck, D.S.O., D.F.C. (2 Bars) Biggin Hill Base, Fighter Command, R.A.F.

It had been compiled by M.I.9, a department of the British Directorate of Military Intelligence, on 3rd May 1945. The source of the photocopied report was a social media friend called Jason Warr, an avid follower of the Stalag Luft 3 story and possessor of a collection of artefacts and memorabilia that would grace any museum.

A little research soon revealed that Wing Commander 'Bob' Stanford-Tuck had been a fighter pilot and Battle of Britain flying ace, credited with downing at least 29 enemy aircraft before his Spitfire was shot down over France in January 1942. That's how he ended up in Stalag Luft 3. With his carefree smile, chiseled features, dark, swept-back hair, and pencil-thin moustache, he was the very epitome of a dashing RAF hero. He was also a key figure in the X Organisation and a close associate of Roger Bushell – Big X.

The documents I now had in my hand contained his detailed description of the delousing party escape, which, as I soon learned, he had helped to plan and then play a key part in.

It was simple opportunism. Personal hygiene facilities in the camp were severely limited, with prisoners only allowed one brief hot shower a week. Sanitation and plumbing was rudimentary, and insect infestations were hard to avoid, especially of lice. Tiny parasites that attach themselves to the skin and live on human blood, lice thrive in dirty and overcrowded conditions and carry serious diseases like typhus. The Germans hated them. If they found an outbreak, they would immediately evacuate the infected hut and set about treating it and all its occupants with delousing insecticide. This involved marching groups of twenty-six prisoners at a time through the main gate of the North Compound, along the outer perimeter road, to the delousing block which was situated by the East Compound.

Roger Bushell and Stanford-Tuck, sensing a chance that was a too good miss, hatched a cunning plan more than worthy of Blackadder's Baldrick: substitute the two German guards that were sent to escort each group of prisoners to the delousing block with two Allied airmen disguised as guards, equip them with a forged gate pass and pretend rifles and spring twenty-six men to freedom. What could possibly go wrong?

Quite a lot.

It required careful preparation. To pass off the substitute guards as the real thing and get them through the gate in broad daylight without arousing suspicion would not be easy. Sagan's escape organisation had carefully pieced together a network of highly skilled kriegies who, between them, could forge just about anything out of almost nothing. There were needleworkers, already well practiced at creating elaborate costumes for the camp's theatre productions, for whom a replica guard's tunic presented a challenge, but not an insurmountable one. All sorts of items were obtained by gaining the confidence of individual guards and then blackmailing them. The X organisation had a team of kriegies who were highly skilled in the art of compromising the integrity of any guards they saw as a soft touch. It took time, often starting with feigned friendship, helped along with gifts of cigarettes, coffee, and chocolate, courtesy of the Red Cross parcels. It only needed one favour coming back the other way to start a process that the victim could not reverse. Any threat of reporting the irregular activity to the camp authorities was enough to ensure an ongoing supply of ever more incriminating favours. No guard wanted to be sent to the Russian front; it was seen as an almost certain death sentence. They knew all too well about the carnage at Stalingrad.

Forging a gate pass required the acquisition of an original to copy, and that meant calling in a favour from one of the compromised guards. It was only needed for a short time; the victim would be assured – that's all it took to create a replica so good as to be virtually indistinguishable from the real thing.

Then there were the dummy rifles; they had to be visually correct in every detail to fool the vigilant Germans. It is said that homemade calipers were used to gauge the exact dimensions; as one prisoner engaged a guard in conversation, another sidled up from behind to take the necessary measurements. It took a few attempts to complete the task. Bed boards were then glued together, carved to the required shape, and burnished with shoe polish until the correct patina was achieved. Metal parts were carefully crafted from whatever odds and ends were to hand. The final result was so convincing that only by handling the imitations could the subterfuge be discovered.

Once the fake metal buttons and insignias for the uniforms had been made and attached, everything was in place to launch the escape. All it needed was a lice infestation, and reporting that was the easy bit; lice or no lice. The hut chosen for the spurious report was Hut 109 – my father's hut.

Two German-speaking airmen, one Belgian, the other Dutch, were lined up to don the uniforms and escort the chosen escapees through the two perimeter gates and out into the pine trees, marching them along the gravel road towards the East Compound delousing block at which, of course, they would never arrive – all being well.

Just as the plan was ready to launch, a major flaw was discovered: the genuine guards were no longer armed with rifles but pistols, back to the drawing board. Holsters were hurriedly fashioned from cardboard and made to look like leather with numerous applications of black boot polish. Pistol butts were carved from yet more bed boards and placed in the holsters, which were stuffed with paper to bulk them out. Once again, all was set to go.

There was one other part to the plan: a decoy party of senior officers, including Bob Stanford-Tuck, would follow almost immediately behind the main escape party in order to divert the attention of the guard in the sentry tower near the gate, who otherwise would have a clear view of the perimeter road between the two compounds. This, it was hoped, would stop the escape into the woods from being spotted. If all went to plan, the party of senior officers would escape as well.

It was a hot, sun-drenched June afternoon when the twenty-six men and fake guards, all handpicked by Big X for their escape abilities, lined up to make their bid for freedom. 'Ginger' Garwell was one of them. Each kriegie carried a small pack containing not blankets and clothing for delousing but a set of freshly tailored civilian clothes along with fake documents, some dried food, and a small amount of German money. All set. The atmosphere was tense. Nervous laughter rang out - a few joshed about. Even a genuine visit to the delousing block was a welcome relief from camp tedium - this was even better. These were men well used to the stomach-churning anticipation of a bombing raid or an aerial dog fight with the enemy; they could easily handle this adrenaline rush.

At 2 pm, the main escape party headed for the North Compound gate with the two fake guards, looking as officious as possible, in close attendance. Stalag Luft 3 was a huge camp with thousands of inmates and hundreds of guards, so the new faces in impeccable-looking counterfeit uniforms raised no suspicions when they presented their fake pass to the sentry on gate duty. He gave it not much more than a cursory glance and waved them through. It was that easy. They turned right and set off towards the East Compound, some 200 metres away.

Meanwhile, the decoy party of five senior Allied officers

approached the gatehouse. They had forged paperwork purporting to authorise a meeting with the camp Commandant, von Lindeiner, on the pretense of needing to discuss some business relating to the supply of Red Cross parcels. Leading the way was a highly decorated Dutch fighter pilot called Bram van der Stok, attired in a faultless copy of a Luftwaffe Unterofficier's uniform. The first gate sentry examined his fake paperwork and waved the party through, but the sentry at the second gate, not recognising this new Unterofficier, grew suspicious. Van der Stok was escorted to the nearby guardroom for questioning while the remaining five senior officers were held between the two gates. As expected, the sentry in the guard tower was watching them and not the perimeter road. Tension mounted.

The first escape party had marched just a short distance when one of the escorting guards looked back and saw Bram van der Stok being led to the guardhouse. Realising that things might be going badly wrong, he swiftly marched the men left and onto a haulage track that led away from the perimeter road. After some seventy metres, the party split into pairs and rapidly melted into the protective cover of Sagan's dark green pine forest. The two fake guards stopped briefly to tear off their German tunics and change into civvies. Then they were gone.

Events in the guardroom were now developing rapidly; a telephone call to the head of camp security in the German Officers' Mess immediately aroused suspicions - nothing was known of a meeting between the senior Allied Officers and the camp Commandant. Security staff rushed to the gate of the North Compound and demanded that the waiting officers be brought into the guardroom and strip-searched. According to Stanford-

Tuck's eyewitness account, he had just enough time to throw his false papers back into the compound to prevent them from being discovered.

The head of security could now afford to gloat, stating that it was useless for any prisoner to attempt escape. Stanford-Tuck agreed, all the while knowing just how wrong he was about to be proved. Just then, with perfect timing, the guardroom telephone rang. The news that a large delousing party had failed to arrive at the East Compound was met with a brief stunned silence. At that precise moment, the camp Commandant, von Lindeiner, burst, red-faced, through the door. When he realised what had happened, that the Allied officers had been acting as a decoy for a much larger escape, he was incandescent with rage and held Stanford-Tuck personally responsible, telling him that his days were numbered.

As the word went out that the first group had not arrived at the delousing station, panic ensued. Suddenly sirens were wailing, dogs were barking, and guards were running from all directions. The search was frantic, with every available member of the camp's personnel sent out to comb the pine forests and beyond. The whole of Germany's security apparatus was put on the highest alert. It was even announced on national radio.

Most of the escapees didn't get far. Some made it to the nearby station, where they hoped to jump on a train. Others hid in the trees, waiting for night to fall. Two - Lorne Welch and Peter Morison - found their way to a nearby aerodrome, where, dressed in replica Luftwaffe uniforms, they attempted to steal a small plane and fly to Switzerland. They were caught and threatened with execution for espionage and for wearing a German uniform but were finally sent to the notorious prison camp at Colditz Castle. Eventually, all of the escapers were recaptured and returned to custody.

And that's how 'Ginger' Garwell ended up in a cell in what the kriegies called the cooler. He was found and arrested just one day after escaping. The Germans initially threatened him with court martial for sabotage and espionage but finally sentenced him to 56 days in solitary confinement - it ran from 12th June through to 8th August 1943.

Somewhere in my distant childhood memory, I can recall seeing a picture - a hand-painted cartoon - depicting one of the escapees peering out from behind a tree trunk as a guard, wielding a rifle, searches in the gloom. I've no idea where it came from or where it went, but I vaguely recall my mum saying to me, *"That was your dad."*

In one way, the attempt could have been seen as a failure since no one had escaped for good, but to Roger Bushell and Bob Stanford-Tuck, it was a great success; the Germans had been fooled and, better still, embarrassed. With thousands of troops ordered to search for the escapees, it had tied up their resources and created mayhem - and all the while, the tunnel digging went on, undiscovered.

The cooler block sat just outside the North Compound's main fence in an administration area called the Vorlager, which also housed the medical facilities. The cells were cramped and bare with just a bed, a small table, and a chair. A tiny window let in some light, but wooden slats prevented any view of the outside world, so there was nothing to see but blank walls. Books were not allowed, nor were cigarettes. It was a bleak place to spend any time, let alone 56 days. Arthur, already as thin as a greyhound, had to survive on meagre rations of watery soup, a little black bread, and maybe a few potatoes. The luxury of Red Cross provisions was banned for the duration. A visit to the toilet required the escort of a guard.

To relieve the seemingly endless hours of tedium, there was, it appears, the opportunity to send and receive some mail. The letter Arthur sent to his family back in Hexham on 29th June 1943, after seventeen days in his cell, gives no hint as to his situation - he was more interested in news of his sister's wedding:

'Dear Family,

I have received several letters from you since last I wrote. News in all of them was very cheering except that about poor old Vic. I shall miss her greeting when I get back. You must get another little dog to take her place.

Well, at this moment, Bee will doubtless be having the time of her life. I am glad, and I am sure that Ron will take good care of her and make her happy. You must write and tell me how things went and send me some photographs. Bee isn't a very good writer, I fear. I shall find it most queer to write to Mrs Curtis! You know, it is a good thing they did not wait for Joan and me. It would have been silly and maybe a rather long business.

My other little sister seems to be doing remarkably well. I was, of course, delighted with the news. She seems to have done it with quite a bit to spare – which is more than I did if you remember!

Now, before I run out of space, would you please hold back one of those fivers you put in War Savings for me and let Joan have it for her birthday, which is somewhere around August 15th? I have a feeling that she may be a bit short of cash at her new job. If you can think of a suitable present - get it though by all means. This saves me writing to the bank. Hope you are fit and well. I am fine.

Love.

Arthur.

P.S. Please send pyjamas.'

Shortly after he wrote this letter, on 13th July 1943, Squadron Leader John Nettleton, recently married and the only pilot from 44 Squadron fortunate enough to get back in one piece from the Augsburg raid, finally ran out of luck. Returning from a night-time raid on Turin in northern Italy, his Lancaster was intercepted by German fighters over the Bay of Biscay soon after daybreak and shot down without trace. His body was never recovered. Of course, Arthur, cooped up in his tiny cell, knew nothing of this, but he would have known that Stalag Luft 3 was a far safer place to be than the cockpit of a bomber.

*Wedding photo taken at 'Viewlands.' Joan
and young Nora are on the right.*

He writes again on July 25th:

'*Dear Family,*

*So far this month, I have received two letters from you on May 27th
and June 15th. I had a letter from Joan some time ago giving an
account of the wedding. Everything seems to have gone off very well,
I was glad to hear. You must have had a tremendous job with all the
arrangements, etc. I have written to Ron and Bee addressing the letter
to you.*

You will be glad to hear that I have at last received my uniform. I was beginning to think that it must be draped around some codfish or other at the bottom of the sea. The only thing I seem to be short of now is underwear (summer), oh yes, and pyjamas. Apart from these articles, I am very nicely equipped.

You ask in your letter about this Flight Lieutenant business. In the RAF, we receive automatic promotion up to F/LT even if you are a POW. Mine became due on April 9th this year. Actually, I had been recommended for an acting F/LT early in April last year but owing to the fact that I was shot down and forced to reside over here before it came through, it was, of course, washed out. However, don't worry about it. My bank account will show when it has come through. My POW number is still 117, by the way. The Germans write a seven with a line through the middle.

Many thanks for the books which are on the way, I am informed by the Red Cross. I am enclosing a photograph. I hope you are keeping fit and happy. I am very well myself.

All love.

Arthur.'

Two weeks after writing this letter, he was released from the cooler and reunited with his mates in Hut 109, little imagining that he would be back inside before the year was out.

CHAPTER 17

Laurel and Hardy – and Girls

I had noticed that in my mother's small collection of group photographs taken at the camp, her Arthur was almost always next to the same man, and, from the names written in pencil on the reverse of each tiny black and white image, I learned that the man in question was called John Cordwell. They shared Room 7 in Hut 109 and were obviously the best of friends. I wanted to find out more.

Standing L-R: Forfar, Hughes, Davidson, Cordwell, Garwell. Seated: Jessop, unknown, Ramsay.

I'd been in touch with Kelvin Youngs, the administrator of a website (*www.aircrewremembered.com*), who has painstakingly put together an online record covering the exploits of WW2 airmen – hundreds of them, including my father and, as I discovered, John Cordwell. I sent Kelvin copies of photographs taken at Stalag Luft 3 showing the two men standing together, and he added them to the website. I soon learned what had led to John Cordwell's capture and imprisonment. It all started with a low-level raid to attack a belt of enemy searchlights at Aachen, a German city to the west of Cologne, on Friday 7th November 1941. Pilot Officer John D. Cordwell, an aspiring young architect, was the observer in Hampden P1201 of 455 Squadron, Royal Australian Air Force. The target was located, and the mission accomplished, but trouble started as soon as the Hampden and its crew of four headed for home. They encountered freak weather conditions and before long, still flying at a low level, were badly off course and heading, almost blind, into the foothills of the Ardennes. They had no chance of seeing the tall chimney stack in their path before it smashed through the Hampden's lower fuselage, severing the fuel lines and causing the engines to cut out. The Australian pilot, Pilot Officer James Gordon, crash-landed the burning aircraft in the dark, close to a village called Onoz, near to the Belgian city of Namur and its famous medieval fortress. Three of the crew struggled free of the wreckage, but John Cordwell was still trapped inside the nose and trying desperately to escape. James Gordon, seeing his plight, climbed back onto the wing and, amidst the flames, showed him how to get out. *"Am I dead?"* Cordwell asked as he emerged coughing and choking. *"Not if I can help it,"* Gordon replied. By some near miracle, all four of the young crew survived despite suffering burns. They were taken in and cared for by the Alexis family, who lived next to the crash site but only until the following day when German soldiers arrived and took them into custody. That's how my father's best pal ended up in Stalag Luft 3.

The next bit came as a real surprise; Kelvin Youngs thought he might be able to put me in touch with one of the Cordwell family – could I leave it with him? The man who he thought might be able to broker the connection was the son of James Gordon, the Hampden pilot. I didn't have to wait long before an email arrived:

'Hi John and Colin,

I believe that you two have a lot to talk about!!!

Very best regards,

Drew Gordon.

Melbourne Australia.'

I sent Colin an email and soon got a reply:

'Dear John,

A tremendous pleasure to hear from you, I tell you! I have heard stories of your father over the years and will be more than happy to fill you in. I live in Chicago, Illinois, U.S.A. Dad was from the southeast end of London, and my mother was a Yank.

I own an English pub in Chicago called the Red Lion. I've owned it for 32 years and within the last two years, have refurbished the place. Upon reopening, I have turned the place into the Imperial War Museum West. I have a section dedicated to the Great Escape, with drawings my father had done while in Stalag Luft 3. Among the pictures is a drawing my father did of your dad's Lanc coming down in the city of Augsburg. There is also a portrait of your father on the wall. I will fill you in on stories of your father if you like. Stay in touch.

All the best,

Colin Cordwell.'

I was amazed and excited all at once. A picture of my dad on the wall of a pub in Chicago? I would never have known without Kelvin's help and the marvel that is the internet. Colin had plenty of stories to share, and more soon followed:

'Our fathers had a special bond. My dad said they were like Laurel and Hardy; they did everything together.

Dad told me that one day, yours and mine went for a walk around the perimeter of the camp. As they walked along the wire, two women came out of the woods and walked parallel with them. One of the women turned to them and said, "Good morning, gentlemen," and they continued their way.

My father said it was a psychological blow that was comparable to being shot. After the walk, my father realized how long it had been since he had been in the company of women. He went back to Hut 109 and lay down for a day, trying to gather his wits.

Later, my father conjectured that it was a planned attempt on the part of the Jerries to help break them down psychologically. Perhaps.'

Thousands of young men confined at close quarters for years on end with nothing but occasional letters and photographs from wives or girlfriends back home were bound to feel pangs of frustration. It seems that seeing real women so close but so far away had a profound effect on young John Cordwell and his pal, Arthur - for a while, at least.

The first letter I possess from my father to his own girl back home is dated 28th November 1943, some 19 months after he last saw her. He'd have written many more before this, but, for whatever reason, none of them was in my mother's old, crumpled carrier bag of memories. Thinking of the future, he wrote:

'Darling Joan,

Here I am again, with, as usual, not much to say, I'm afraid. I only hope that I'm back to you before you get this letter. We have received some information by mail about possible conditions at the end of the war. I believe that we are supposed to get three months' leave with pay before being recalled for possible further training – though I think there should be a fair amount of demobilisation (I hope!) I like the sound of three months' leave, don't you? That should give us bags of time to get married and have a honeymoon of about three months! You know, on thinking things over, I find that I have hardly any ideas at all about plans. I shall, in all probability, be in such a daze when I get back that you will have to lead me about like a child!!

Two things are clear to me – that we have wasted enough of this life writing to each other at a range of about 700 miles and so should waste no time in remedying that evil and getting married (I bet you agree with that, don't you?). The other point is that, if it should be possible and you like the idea, we should go over to S. Africa. That would probably not be possible for at least a year after the war, if at all. Even then, I suppose this last idea might easily change after a month or two back to normal. In fact, darling, the only thing that is clear is that I love you very much. We shall no doubt have plenty of time on our leave to work out and discuss plans. I'm sorry, our reunion will, in all probability, not be till after Christmas. Let us hope it will be very early in the New Year.'

Why would a lad from rural Northumberland be thinking of a future in Africa? Well, he was attached to 44 'Rhodesia' Squadron and so had pals who spoke highly of the life they enjoyed in the colonies there – some of his roommates in Hut 109 too. He would return to the idea in later letters to Joan. Africa might have to wait, but one thing he wasn't going to postpone was their marriage – that would happen just as soon as possible. Both of these hopes would come to be realised, but only one of them in the way he anticipated:

'I suppose that by the time you receive this, the winter will be almost over, and you will be getting ready for swimming and tennis again! I hope and trust that you are keeping fit and well and above all happy.

Ever yours, darling.

Arthur.'

Romance was in the air for his sister, Beatrice, too. A couple of months earlier, he had written home:

'Dear Family, since I wrote to you last, I have received two letters from you, one from Nora and the other containing the first of the wedding photographs. I was delighted with the snap. Bee must have been a very charming bride. It was very nice to see you, Dad, after so long. My collection of the family is now complete.

Everything is going pretty well here. This week I have had my first cold since I arrived. I am pretty well fixed up for cigarettes, clothes, etc. I had 200 Craven 'A' yesterday from someone by the name of W. Nicholson. Do you know of anyone of that name?'

It seems his parents were letting him know about local war casualties:

'I was sorry to hear about R. Martin. I am afraid that Frank Brown is not here. I have kept an eye open for him. By the way, have you ever heard again from Mr Edwards, father of one of my crew? I wondered if he had definite news from the Red Cross...'

Sergeant Ivor Edwards, aged just 22, son of Joseph and Mary Edwards of Newbridge, Monmouthshire, had died in the rear gun turret of Lancaster R5510, consumed by flames. His poor mother and father wanted, at least, to know where he had been buried and were desperately anxious for news. Arthur's parents knew they could so easily have been in the same sad situation. His resting place is known now: Plot 6G6 at Durnbach War Cemetery, Germany. I hope they found out.

The letter concludes on a lighter note:

'Well, I hope that you are getting the larder pretty well stocked up for a mighty Christmas dinner. I think that there's a tiny chance that I might share it with you. Love to you all, Arthur.'

'A tiny chance that I might share it with you.' – Was he thinking of escaping again?

The entrance to escape tunnel 'Tom' in Hut 123 had just been discovered, completely by chance. German suspicions had been aroused when they found a Red Cross box filled with freshly excavated sand. During the intensive search that followed, one of the ferrets had accidentally dropped his metal probe right by the concrete slab that concealed the tunnel's entry shaft. Bending down to pick it up, he noticed a slight irregularity in the surface and started scratching at it. That's all it took. The

Germans were jubilant. When they found out the depth of the tunnel, they decided that the only sure way of demolishing it was to detonate explosive charges along its length. Hut 123 was cleared, and a large group of kriegies gathered at a safe distance to watch months of gruelling work go up in smoke. But tunnel Tom had one last trick up its sleeve; to minimise blast damage to the hut, the guards had decided to put the concrete slab back in the entrance before detonating the charges. It was a mistake. When the explosion came, it blew the slab straight through the hut roof and into the sky, where it described a graceful arc before smashing back through another part of the roof to the loud cheers of the assembled kriegies. Laurel and Hardy would have approved.

One tunnel had gone, and another, 'Dick,' which ran parallel to it, had been mothballed, which left tunnel 'Harry' in Hut 104 as the focus of X Organisation's full energy. With the Germans never imagining that other tunnels existed and believing they could now relax their guard just a little, escape preparations resumed in earnest.

CHAPTER 18

A Christmas Caper

On Monday 1ˢᵗ November 1943, Ginger Garwell, John Cordwell, and the rest of the inmates of Room 7, Hut 109, welcomed a new arrival. It was the end of a very long, harrowing journey for Flight Lieutenant Ken Carson, a tall, dark-haired Australian fighter pilot.

The journey had started in North Africa, not far from the Libyan port city of Tobruk on the Mediterranean coast. The battle of the Western Desert was raging. British forces had captured the city from the Italians at the beginning of 1941 but then moved on to fight battles in Greece and Syria, leaving a skeleton force of poorly equipped Australian and British troops to defend the port. German armies commanded by General Rommel laid siege to the city from April but, meeting dogged resistance, were unable to recapture it. The Luftwaffe piled into the battle with aerial bombing raids supported by its formidable Messerschmitt Bf 109 fighter aircraft.

Newly trained and just twenty-one years old, Ken Carson was pitched headlong into the conflict, piloting the American-built Curtiss Kittyhawk fighter, adorned with its garish sharks-teeth livery, in deadly combat with the enemy. By November, he had downed his first Bf 109 just before the Allied Eighth Army broke the siege and relieved the trapped garrison in Tobruk. But the dogfights, high in the clear blue African skies, continued. In

December, he was shot up but successfully landed his damaged aircraft. In January 1942, he had to crash-land after a hail of cannon fire from a Bf 109 hit the Kittyhawk. In February, he downed his second Bf 109. In March, he was promoted to Flight Lieutenant. Then, in June, his aircraft was shot down by ground fire. It plummeted into the desert sands in flames.

Soldiers from Rommel's Afrika Korps quickly pulled him, badly injured, from the burning wreckage. He was taken to a German field hospital before being flown to Benghazi and then transferred to a hospital ship bound for the Italian port of Naples. Next stop was a hospital in nearby Caserta where he could receive better treatment for his wounds. He was there for four months. Then came a 700-kilometer rail journey to a convalescent hospital in Bergamo, near Milan, to be cared for by nuns. While he was there, a field dressing, still embedded in his thigh, had to be surgically removed.

When sufficiently recovered, he was moved through a succession of prisoner-of-war camps in Italy until, in September 1943, the Italians surrendered to the Allies. Hitler's armies then took over control of the country from Mussolini, and Ken was taken north by rail to Germany along with hundreds of other POWs. They were crowded into boxcars with very little food or water and no sanitation. Ken was held in camps at Munich and Strasbourg until, finally, he arrived at Stalag Luft 3 and Hut 109, sixteen months after being shot down.

Every inmate of Stalag Luft 3 was lucky to be alive, and, like young Ken Carson, every one of them had a story to tell.

With Christmas approaching and the tide of war slowly turning in favour of the Allied forces, Arthur sent this postcard home. His hopes of an early homecoming were running high:

'Dear Family,

Just a line to let you know I'm fit & well. Should be seeing you in a few months, I hope. Have had very little mail this month, but I believe there's a holdup somewhere. Could you please send a couple of quid to Mrs J.H. Mann, Hundon Cottages, Ashley, Nr Newmarket, Suffolk for Christmas. She is the wife of our room orderly – a very good fellow, and as we have no money here, I feel this would be a nice way of acknowledging the hard work he does for us. Wishing you all a happy time this Christmas. Love. Arthur.'

Reading this, I wondered about the role of the room orderly. What exactly was it? Who might fulfil it? I put these questions to an online group that is crammed with Stalag Luft 3 experts. The answer came quickly: just some of the duties of an orderly were to sweep the room and hallway, clean the dinner table, wash the dishes, do the laundry, fetch water and food rations, and feed the stove in winter (fuel permitting) peel spuds (if there were any) shine shoes, mend clothing and make tea in the early morning. No wonder Mrs Mann was getting a couple of quid for Christmas. Her husband, whose efforts were so appreciated, would have been a private or someone of lower rank who volunteered for the job in the belief that he'd be better off being locked up with a bunch of relatively privileged officers than risking a harsher regime elsewhere.

The camp was continually expanding as more and more POWs, including the new influx of prisoners from Italy, arrived. The bunk beds in an already cramped Room 7 were shuffled round to make room for Flight Lieutenant Carson, so J.H. Mann had even more plates to wash.

Camp life was likely a little surprising to new arrivals. It's doubtful they expected to find a fully functioning theatre or see the latest films from Hollywood, or play in a football league, but that's how it was, according to this extract from one of Arthur's letters to his mum and dad, sent during that October:

'Well, winter is now coming on rapidly. Our garden is finished. It yielded a good crop of tomatoes. The theatre is now in full swing. Have seen four very good shows and we are expecting our first English film tomorrow. This will be the first since I was shot down. Ginger Rogers and Fred Astaire in "Shall We Dance." We have a fine soccer Association running now. I am playing for Arsenal in the first league. Have won both our matches 3-0 & 6-0.

Cheerio. All my love. I am very fit and well. Arthur.'

By the end of November, the expected freezing weather had not yet arrived, and preparations for another Christmas in captivity were underway. In the middle of writing his next letter home, Arthur makes this comment:

'I have broken off here to examine a very fine cake made by a fellow in the room, F/LT Michell (Rhodesian cricketer). The standard of cooking here is amazingly high! (I've known it pretty low too on occasions).'

It was possibly a Christmas cake, but he doesn't say. He continues:

'Many thanks for the parcel which I received this month. Everything was ok except for the mug, which was unfortunately broken. I also received Penguin books some time ago and now have all the last batch

of gramophone records. Snaps all came through, and I thought them very good. I received your message about the bank balance & pay ok. The blanket you ask about is doing fine service. So far, we have had no weather cold enough to cause any worry. Time seems to fly past. One day you look at the calendar & note the date & then the next time you look, a couple of months have gone past!

No, I do not play the accordion. I did, till the blokes in the room got fed up! Been playing more soccer recently. We played six games, won three, drew three & stood at the top of the table, but only just. Expecting to try some ice skating soon. Not very successful last year - too wearing on my pants. In general, I'm keeping very well and pretty happy. Hope to see you before Christmas '44. Cheerio, Love, Arthur.'

Ice skating? Apparently so. In the middle of each compound was a large square pool full of water for use in the event of a fire. In summer, it doubled up as a swimming pool and, in the winter, a skating rink. Sport, theatre, cinema, escaping – there was plenty to keep kriegies busy.

Something else was no doubt being prepared for Christmas, something without which Christmas just wouldn't feel right – alcohol. 'Hooch,' they called it; a fiery, home-brewed concoction, strong enough in only moderate quantities to lay a man out. It was typically made from dried fruit or potato, which was fermented and distilled into a potent spirit. It was illicit, of course, as was much else that went on under German noses, and was reserved for very special occasions.

The story of what happened that Christmas I would never have known but, once again, for the internet. I'd shared a small black and white photograph taken in Room 7, Hut 109, with an online

group called 'Stalag Luft 3 – The Great Escape – Prisoners of War.'
The photo shows a wall decorated with kriegie artwork and,
somewhat surprisingly, a homemade cuckoo clock. Six men face
the camera. My father is sitting in front left, his legs nonchalantly
crossed, a lit cigarette in his right hand. He looks so young. John
Cordwell, sporting a moustache, is standing behind him. To the
right of the group, hands in pockets stands Ken Carson. I knew
nothing about him then, just that his name, along with those of
the others, was written in pencil on the reverse of the photograph.
I was soon to find out more – a lot more.

*Room seven friends. Standing: Cordwell, Michell, Van Toen, Carson.
Seated: Garwell, Samson. Van Toen's homemade cuckoo clock
is on the wall. An accordion can be seen on the floor.*

The photograph, dated February 1944, was signed by each man:

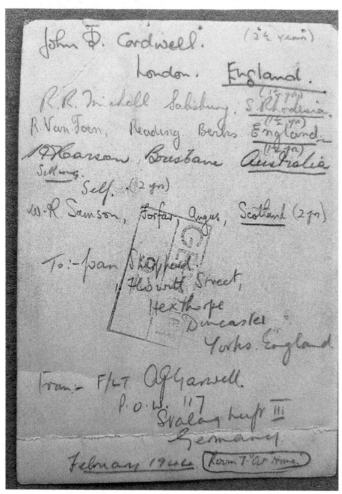

It was stamped on the back by censor 90. Thanks to my friend Ben van Drogenbroek, an expert on the history of Stalag Luft 3, I know her name, Sigrid Moritz. This is a photograph of her:

The first communication I had with John Carson, Ken's son, came through the same online group. He'd seen the photo and instantly recognised his dad standing there. So now I was in touch with two sons of Room 7 inmates, one in America, and the other, John, in Australia. John and I began to piece together the dramatic events of that Christmas.

I already knew that my father had endured a second stretch of solitary confinement in the North Compound cooler between the 26th of December and the 17th of January but had no idea why. The dates didn't coincide with any escape that I knew of, organised or otherwise. Then I received an email from John that provided my first real clue. He told me about a conversation he'd had with his dad back in 2002 when they were seated together watching, once again, a rerun of 'The Great Escape' on TV. Picking up on one of the many inaccuracies in the narrative, Ken suddenly muttered under his breath, *"The cooler was nothing like that."* He then proceeded to tell his son a story that he had never told a soul in almost sixty years; how he and an unnamed mate had drunk this lethal home-brewed hooch and decided to let off steam by clambering over the fence separating their compound from the American compound. He recalled gunfire in the darkness and sparks flying off the barbed wire but, somehow, making it over without injury. And he remembered being discovered in the wrong compound during the following day's roll call and ending up in the cooler. His son, John, was so amazed at the story that he found himself momentarily doubting its truthfulness.

John concluded his email to me by asking: *'Could it be your own father who figures as the other fellow in the fence jumping caper?'* That set me thinking about the date of Arthur's second stretch in the cooler – 26th December, the day after Christmas, just the time of year when kriegies might enjoy the liberating effects of too much alcohol. It seemed to fit.

Not long after, it all fell into place, thanks to a book about Stalag Luft 3 written by Ben van Drogenbroek and Steve Martin entitled 'The Camera Became My Passport Home.' In the book, I came across the translation of a letter written by the camp Commandant, Colonel von Lindeiner-Wildau, and addressed to the senior allied officers of the three compounds, North, East, and South. Dated 27th December 1943, it read:

'On my return here, I have established with regret that, in spite of my most earnest admonitions, the trust which was placed in the POWs, the way in which requests were met halfway, and the special concessions given to the POWs, over the Christmas holidays have led to intolerable incidents.

1. *Nine British POWs of North Camp climbed the barbed wire fence separating North and South Camps on the night of 25/26th.*
2. *On the night of 25/26th, 13 POWs of the U.S.A.A.F. climbed without permission the barbed wire fence separating the South from the North Camp.*
3. *On the night of 25/26th, 3 British POWs of East Camp climbed the barbed wire fence separating East and Centre without permission.*

I am punishing the officers concerned with 14 days' close arrest. The sentence is to begin on 26/12/43. The special privileges allowed in connection with the close of the year are hereby withdrawn.'

The final paragraph clinched it for me:

'The possession and use of drinks containing alcohol is forbidden with effect from today, instead of as hitherto ordered with effect from 4/1/44. Existing alcohol will be confiscated and destroyed.

(Signed) Von Lindeiner, Colonel, and Commandant.'

So that was it; with any sense of fear banished under the influence of kriegie hooch and with no thought to the possible consequences, Arthur, Ken, and seven others decided it would be a hoot to clamber over to the American compound on that cold, dark, Christmas night. They could so easily have been shot.

Cooped up in the cooler again, Arthur had plenty of time to write home. In a letter dated 28th December, just a couple of days after his alcohol-fuelled adventure, it's as if nothing at all had happened:

'Dear Family - Many thanks for your letter of November 2nd, which reached me on Dec 21st. I was glad to hear that you are all well. You must find life comparatively peaceful these days with two of the family off your hands and Nora growing up. Ron and Bee seem to have had a very good holiday. I don't hear from them very often, but I gather that they are both very happy. Did you have Joan up for Christmas?

Christmas here went very well. We had all the food we could eat, thanks to the Red Cross. We are looking forward with confidence to the new year. Hope to see you by about August. Time goes so quickly that that doesn't really seem very long. Cigarette parcels come through very slowly, but I get enough to keep going. Most of my letters go to Joan these days, so you probably find them few and far between. I know that you will understand & forgive me. Cheerio now. Love to you all. Arthur.'

And so, 1943 drew to a close. It had not been short of an adventure for prisoner 117. He knew how the war was going and expected to be free before another Christmas passed, but he knew nothing of the dark turn of events about to unfold at Stalag Luft 3.

CHAPTER 19

The Great Escape

A January night; freezing air licks around the corners of the camp's wooden huts as wisps of smoke drift lazily up from a hundred stoves. One by one, windows dim to darkness, and all falls silent. Frost spreads its white tentacles across the dark expanse of open ground, through the perimeter fence, and into the sleeping forest beyond. Searchlights sweep the silence with probing eyes. As another long day in solitary confinement nears its end, Arthur Garwell tries to settle on the cold, hard bed in his cell and find some sleep. Below him, hidden deep beneath nine metres of sandy soil, lies tunnel Harry, waiting in silence.

Roger Bushell, Big X, had decided that it was now safe enough to restart tunnelling operations. The entrance to Harry was reopened, and the shaft was examined for any signs of deterioration since the discovery and destruction of tunnel Tom had halted digging two months earlier. Apart from needing some minor repairs, all seemed good to go. Now around thirty metres long, a halfway house was constructed where the tunnellers could change from one wooden railway trolley to another on their journeys to and from the tunnel face. It was named 'Piccadilly,' after the London Underground station. By all reckoning, it lay directly below the cooler where Arthur was paying the price for his Christmas boozing escapade.

Some 600 men were, in some way or another, involved in the massive, covert operation. It wasn't just about digging; every one of the proposed 200 escapees had to be equipped with civilian clothing, maps, a compass, forged documents, money, and a strong alibi. They had to know where they were going and, if stopped, why. The ingenuity needed to produce so much material from the little that could be gleaned in a prison camp was, without exaggeration, astounding. Everything had to be hidden away from the prying eyes of the guards, who could arrive and search without warning at any time. Kriegie stooges kept a constant lookout. Tension mounted.

On 17th January 1944, freed from the cooler, Arthur re-joined his mates in Hut 109. Next door was Hut 104 and the entrance to tunnel Harry. Beyond that stood two perimeter fences, the forest, and, for some, an uncertain future.

His next letter home is dated the 22nd of February:

> *'Dear Family, Since I wrote last, I have received six letters from you written between Nov. 16th and Jan. 6th. You seem to have had a quiet though pleasant Christmas. I'm sorry I couldn't be with you. Perhaps for the next one, eh? One of the letters was from Nora. I was delighted to hear that she is doing so splendidly at school. I haven't heard from Ron & Bee for a month or two, but it's probably because I don't write except for the very odd card. I hope they are getting on well. Please give them my sincere regards when you next write. They will have been married a year now.*
>
> *How time flies! If I don't get back soon, I shan't know any of the family except my old mum & dad. By the way, I met an old friend of mine here - a chap I haven't seen for over two years - and he thought*

I looked very well, though a bit thinner in the face. By the way, the records you sent for my birthday arrived in time. I have already received the 10", but not the 12" (though they are here). I have also to thank you for my September clothing parcel, which arrived intact about a month ago. I was particularly glad of the pyjamas as my night attire was anything but respectable! In future parcels, I would like some gramophone needles if you can get them. Please do not send any more collars as I never wear them, and anyway, they usually seem to be too small (probably through my washing!).

We have a little snow here, but things are getting more springlike every day. Looking forward to some sunshine in a few weeks! I made a couple more rugs recently. They are about 3 ft x 1 ½ ft and took me two days each. Another fellow in the room has made a clock out of a few tins, some nails, and a razor blade. It works on the weight system & keeps a pretty good time!! Cheerio. Love. Arthur.'

The clockmaker was Reginald Van Toen - the Room 7 bed-smasher. The clock can be seen on the wall behind him in the group photograph taken that same month.

As the tunnel slowly progressed, the disposal of excavated sand started to become an issue; it was difficult to hide when winter snows covered the ground. The solution was found in, of all places, the camp theatre and the void that lay beneath its seating area. All it took was the creation of a hidden trapdoor under one of the seats and the selection of a crack sand-shifting team of some eighty men. Large bags of sand were lugged laboriously up Harry's nine-meter shaft, then taken across to the next nearest hut - 109 - to be dispersed into bags small enough to conceal under a coat. The remaining journey across the compound to the theatre required the cover of darkness and a lot of care, with the carriers switching routes often to avoid arousing suspicion. Arthur and the men of Room 7, if not involved, would likely have known what was going on.

Progress was rapid, and Harry had soon doubled in length, reaching as far as the outer fence where another changeover station was dug – this one named Leicester Square. Meanwhile, two reels of electrical cable needed to extend the lighting were spirited away from a team of visiting German electricians who, fearing reprisals, failed to report the loss. The ferrets, sensing that something untoward was going on, intensified their searches, still worried that one of the hut stoves might conceal another tunnel entrance. Rooms were turned upside down, suspects were searched, but, despite numerous close calls, nothing incriminating was found.

By the end of February and with the whole plan nearing completion, dark rumours started to circulate. Somehow word had got out that the Gestapo was threatening severe reprisals against any recaptured prisoners should another escape succeed. Was it worth the risk with the war rapidly going the way of the Allies? Some thought not, but with such a massive effort by so many over so long a period finally nearing fruition, any idea of backing out was rapidly pushed aside.

Just over 500 names were entered into a series of draws to see who would get a chance to taste freedom – almost all of them X Organisation workers. Those with the best language skills – and some of them were multilingual – went into the initial draw, their chances of making it all the way home considered the best. They would be first out of the tunnel. At the end of the process, 200 kriegies had one of the coveted tickets, numbered in order of exit. Each man had to have a detailed plan; who would they pair up with? Where would they be heading, and how did they plan to get there? What was their cover story if challenged? Clothing, documents, food, money; every tiny detail had to be considered, every preparation finalised. A few kriegies got cold feet and backed out, one of them realising at the last minute that his claustrophobia was too crippling for a 100-metre journey along a tunnel little wider than a coffin.

By March 14th, the excavations had been completed. By all calculations, the tunnel had reached as far as the forest that lay beyond the outer fence and the perimeter road. It had been a tricky task to dig the vertical exit shaft back up through nine metres of sandy soil with the constant risk of collapse threatening to bury the tunnellers alive, but they had done it. It stopped just short of the surface, where it was capped with wooden slats, ready for the final order to put the whole incredible plan into action.

March 24th was the chosen date, a night with no moon to light up the recently fallen snow. Two hundred men made their way, one by one, to Hut 104, many of them via Arthur's hut - 109. They had to take different routes at carefully selected times to avoid arousing suspicion. Once there, they took pre-allocated bunks, leaving the usual occupants to move huts and bed down wherever the new arrivals had come from. It took most of the day.

By 8 pm, everyone was in position, ready for the word go. The atmosphere in Hut 104 was a fizzy cocktail of excitement and anticipation with just a twist of trepidation. This was it. Two hundred young men, almost all in their early twenties, waited to take the shortest rail trip of their young lives and begin a journey to the destination they all craved - freedom. And if it went wrong? Like others before them, it would likely be a little worse than interrogation and a stretch in the cooler - or so they thought.

Just after 8:30 pm, the first group of men, including Roger Bushell, descended the ladder to the foot of the entry shaft and began, one by one, to crawl into the cramped and claustrophobic tunnel. One man went ahead to climb the exit shaft, remove the capping boards, and break through the last few inches of soil and snow into the cold dark night above. Others took up their positions at Leicester Square and Piccadilly, ready to pull on the ropes that would haul the kriegie-laden trolleys laboriously through 100 metres of dimly lit tunnel to the base of the exit ladder. It did not go exactly to plan. First off, the capping boards, swollen with moisture, wouldn't budge. It took the efforts of two men and almost an hour to free them while down in the tunnel, nerves were beginning to fray. Then, with the last vestiges of soil removed, a solitary head poked slowly and tentatively above the ground, fully expecting to see the protective cover of the forest and lots of tree trunks. Instead, there came the horrifying realisation that, despite all the calculations, the tunnel had come up a full three metres short of the forest when it should have been several metres within it. Not only that, but the exit was also now in full view of a sentry tower with its searchlight, machine gun, and patrolling guard. The head rapidly disappeared again. When the news reached Roger Bushell, there followed a hurried discussion of possible options; suggestions that the attempt be aborted until the tunnel could be extended were considered but quickly brushed aside. Everything was ready. The forged papers were date stamped. It would have to be now.

The first man out crawled to the edge of the forest and hid from view, leaving a rope trailing back to the exit hole. When the snow-covered ground was clear of patrolling guards, two sharp tugs signalled for the second man to emerge. He headed out into the darkness of the woods, trailing another rope to guide those that followed to a rendezvous spot. Now the escape could start in earnest.

Back in Hut 104, tension eased as the rest of the two hundred ticketholders heard the news and began to move slowly through the corridor towards the tunnel. It was supposed to take two or three minutes to pull each man through, but it wasn't easy to lay prostrate on a tiny wooden trolley with outstretched arms like Superman while holding onto a travel case or a blanket roll. There were trolly-stopping collisions that dislodged support boards, almost burying some kriegies in falling sand. Others fell off completely. At one point, the tunnel was plunged into darkness when the electric lights failed after an air raid warning rang out. Everything was taking far longer than predicted, and after three hours, fewer than twenty-five prisoners had reached the forest.

The early escapees had already struck out, trudging through the deep snow to Sagan's railway station, just a couple of kilometres away. There they tried to mingle inconspicuously with other passengers, including a few off-duty camp guards, as they waited impatiently for delayed trains to arrive. Some posed as businessmen, others as foreign workers. One wore a fake Luftwaffe uniform. All of them adopted the calm, confident demeanour which was essential if they were to carry off the subterfuge.

Slowly, one by one, the tunnel disgorged its kriegie contents into the freezing night air. One by one, they crawled across the snow-covered ground to the sheltering trees and made for freedom, but it was taking far too long to have any hope of getting 200 men out before dawn skies started to lighten. Shortly after 5 am, one guard strayed from his usual route around the perimeter fence and headed, unknowingly, straight for the tunnel entrance. There, in clear view, he saw the prone figure of a man lying in the snow. That was the end of it.

Panic and pandemonium ensued. The guard's torch briefly revealed a shocked, upturned face down in the shaft. Everything had to be slammed into reverse as whistles blew and gunshots rang out. Those waiting in the tunnel scrambled back out into Hut 104 and rapidly destroyed all the evidence they possibly could. Once empty of its last few occupants, the entrance shaft was quickly sealed, and the stove, still burning, returned to its place. Men tore off incriminating clothing and made for their bunks. A few fled Hut 104 to try and get back to their original quarters but echoing gunfire soon put a stop to that.

Seventy-six kriegies were now out of Stalag Luft 3 and rapidly scattering in different directions. The earliest escapees, having eventually caught their delayed trains, were already long gone, but those toward the back of the queue faced very different journeys; they were the ones planning to struggle on foot through the knee-deep snow and frozen wastelands of a German winter. They were called the 'hard-arses' and were destined to spend their nights out in the open, stumbling through the darkness in the hope of avoiding detection. Any sleep would have to be found during daylight, maybe holed up in some remote farm outbuilding as they headed for the border and the freedom they craved. Unlike the Steve McQueen character in 'The Great Escape,' no one fled the chasing Germans by jumping a fence on a stolen motorcycle.

CHAPTER 20

The Game's Up

Whoever had the job of breaking the news to Commandant von Lindeiner had an unenviable task. It is said that this normally measured, reasonable man flew into a barely controlled outburst of rage; his craggy features contorted in anger. There would be severe repercussions - he had already warned his charges of that - but he also knew that he himself would be held responsible.

Within an hour of the escape being discovered, Hut 104 was surrounded by a heavily armed riot squad, and the would-be escapers were dragged out at gunpoint, lined up, and ordered to strip to their underwear in the freezing cold. They should have been marched to the cooler, but it couldn't accommodate them all, so most ended up back in their own huts. The compound was thoroughly searched to establish who was missing, and a list was drawn up. It was a longer list than von Lindeiner might have feared - much longer.

News of the escape quickly spread up the Luftwaffe's chain of command and on to the Reich Criminal Police Department - the Kripo. The highest level of national security alert was declared. Rail stations, airfields, and ports were notified. Instructions to search every farm building, every street, and every hotel for miles around were issued. Roads were blocked, and traffic stopped. It could not be allowed to succeed.

Over the following days, in ones and twos, all but three of the escapees were apprehended, including Roger Bushell - Big X - himself. Many were frozen, wet through, and exhausted from their exposure to the elements. Some had suffered frostbite. They expected to be taken back to Stalag Luft 3 but ended up in different prison facilities miles away, where they faced hostile and prolonged interrogation.

Adolf Hitler had been informed of the escape the day after it happened. Flying into one of his characteristic outbursts of volcanic rage, he barked instructions for all recaptured prisoners to be shot. The head of the Luftwaffe, Hermann Göring, urged caution and tried to talk him down. Hitler, though, insisted that, if not all of them, it should be more than half. The bespectacled, ruthless Heinrich Himmler, second in command of the Third Reich and the architect of the Holocaust, decided on fifty, a nice round number. Once the full list of recaptured men reached the Kripo headquarters in Berlin, the fateful selection was made, and the execution orders dispatched. The Geneva Convention, which protected prisoners of war from the death penalty, regardless of the side they fought for, would be ignored.

They were taken from wherever they were imprisoned in small groups and at different times; some were loaded into cars by menacing Gestapo heavies, others into small trucks by Luftwaffe men. They were all handcuffed. None of them knew their destination, but a few feared the worst.

Squadron Leader Roger Bushell and his escape partner, a young French Spitfire pilot, Lieutenant Bernard Scheidhauer, had been among the first men to leave the tunnel and the first to be recaptured. They'd boarded a train at Sagan's railway station posing as French workmen and got as far as Saarbrücken, some 500 miles to the west. It was tantalisingly close to the French border, but when a discrepancy in their documentation was discovered as they waited to board a connecting train, they were arrested and handed over to the local Gestapo. Three days later, they were bundled into a waiting car and driven away. Reaching a wooded area deep into the countryside, the car stopped. Bushell and Scheidhauer were allowed out on the pretext of taking a comfort break; instead, they were shot in the back of the head at close range. They were still in handcuffs.

All fifty of the murdered men met their end in a similar way; a short journey to an unknown destination, ending in summary execution at some lonely roadside. No large groups, just ones, and twos. No warning of their fate, just a nagging fear in the pit of their stomachs, then oblivion.

On 6th April, the Senior British Officer at Stalag Luft 3, Group Captain Herbert Massey, was summoned to a meeting with a newly appointed camp commandant. Colonel von Lindeiner had, as he feared, been held personally responsible for the escape and removed from his post. An awkward silence filled the room before a short communique from the German High Command was read out to Massey. It announced the deaths but claimed that every prisoner had been shot while resisting arrest or trying to escape after arrest. It was an obviously implausible story since not one of them had just been wounded – all of them had died. A deeply shocked Massey angrily demanded that the names be supplied to him and then left.

The news rapidly spread through an incredulous camp. It was all the more horrifying for the seventeen men who had returned to the relative safety of Stalag Luft 3 but had no idea why they had been spared the same fate as their fellow escapees.

Escaping was no longer a game with little more than a stretch in the cooler at risk; even the Luftwaffe guards and the ever-vigilant ferrets were dismayed at the outcome. Only three men got completely away - two Norwegian airmen, Per Bergsland and Jens Müller, who made it to neutral Sweden by train and ship, and Bram van der Stok (he of the failed delousing party escape) who got to the British consulate in Spain with the help of the French Resistance. Six other recaptured men escaped death; two of them ended up in the supposedly impregnable Colditz Castle, and four were sent to Sachsenhausen concentration camp. All survived the war.

The hapless German electricians who lost two reels of cable but failed to report the theft were executed for their error.

CHAPTER 21

A Little Bit of England Appearing Through the Mist

On 24th April 1944 – just over a week after the names of the murdered men had been pinned to the camp notice board for all to see – Arthur Garwell, now two years into his captivity, wrote to his fiancée, Joan Shepherd, at 1 Flowitt Street, Hexthorpe, Doncaster, Yorkshire:

'My darling,

I'm afraid I haven't much to say tonight, but the end of the month is here again, so I must write – though I had hoped to receive some more of your letters before doing so. Nothing much has happened here since I wrote last, except that the weather has been somewhat disappointing.'

'Nothing much has happened here' could not have been further from the truth, but he couldn't tell Joan what had happened even if he wanted to; it would never have escaped the censor's black pen. Instead, he wrote about their plans for the future:

'I am attaching a perspective of the house I wrote about some time ago. It would be wizard to have a small place of our own. We shall one day, I have no doubt, but things may be so unsettled after the war *that it would be impossible for some years. However, there is no harm in thinking about it, is there? I shall look forward to receiving your ideas and criticisms.'*

Having budding architect John Cordwell as a roommate and best friend was an opportunity not to be missed:

'The view shown is from the north and presumably roadside. Most of the window space is, of course, facing south and not shown. The attachment on the west side would be a garage with a gate through, leading to a side door and front of the house.'

That's almost the same configuration as his family home back in Northumberland. He carries on by getting into the details:

'You will notice that there is so far no means of heating water. Johnny & I have had several discussions on this subject (we have nothing else to do!). He has switched the whole layout round in a plan he has done so that the dining room cum lounge fire is at the west side of the room & thus heats water & kitchen on the back to the back system as we have at home. In my opinion (if that's worth anything), this rather spoils the dining room. I favour a gas or electric heating unit in the kitchen – though this is probably more expensive. What do you think? (I hope you are not bored by all this!).'

Recalling fond memories of 'Viewlands,' high up on the hill above Hexham, and dreaming of the future life he hoped to share with Joan went some way to relieving the many long hours of prison camp tedium. But, not wanting to bore his future wife, and maybe realising that he was being a bit sparing on the romantic front, his letter continues:

'Anyway, darling, I'm sure that wherever we live, we shall be very happy together – though I'm sure I'm getting the best of the bargain!

I had a letter from Ron & Bee. Ron wrote it over a cup of coffee prior to returning. They sounded on top of the world and made me green with envy! How I long for our day to come, darling. I sometimes dream that I am with you again, but it's an awful disappointment to wake up and see the same old room staring at you.

All my love,

Arthur.'

While Arthur dreamt about the future, back in Britain, news of the murdered fifty spread far and wide. Anthony Eden, the Foreign Minister, rose in the House of Commons to pledge that those responsible for such a blatant outrage would be brought to justice. Nothing, though, could ease the aching grief of the fifty bereaved families.

Every letter from Arthur that dropped through the letterbox at 'Viewlands' brought fresh comfort to his worried family, but, as the months ticked by, mail was taking longer and longer to arrive. He wrote this letter on April 28th:

'Dear Family,

Many thanks for your letters of 3rd and 28th of February, which reached me this morning. Mail has been coming through very badly this way. I received Mr Gardner's letter of February 22nd some time ago. I regret that owing to the shortage of mail, I am unable to write to him in reply, but please give him and the rest of the staff my thanks and best wishes. I was very sorry to hear the bad news about Hodgson. He was a fine fellow and, as you say, always so cheerful.

Many thanks for the parcel of January 3rd, which reached me on April 13th. About 2 lbs of chocolate was missing. The rest was intact. The sock feet Mum sends I find extremely handy and very satisfactory. I have no particular requests for future parcels except perhaps a couple of new pullovers if you can get them for next winter - though I'm hoping I shan't be here. Cigarette parcels haven't been coming through at all recently. As far as I am concerned, either they are not dispatched by the firms (which I think likely), or they are lost in transit.

You asked about study. I did a fair amount of book-keeping and accountancy around Christmas with a view to taking the Royal Society of Arts exams, but at the last moment, I was prevented from doing so. I don't worry about it very much as I think that the main thing in this life is to keep a fit and healthy body and a reasonably active mind. I do all sorts of odd things - painting and drawing, reading (good novels, French, Shakespeare), and playing soccer now and then. I played in a game for the old Kriegies (POWs two years and over) versus the new the other day. Result: nil-nil. Must say cheerio. I am very fit and well and pretty optimistic, and I trust that you are the same. Arthur.'

That Easter, Joan had been up to stay with Arthur's folks at 'Viewlands' - she took every possible opportunity to be there, soaking up the feeling of a family she'd never had herself. Arthur sent her a postcard:

'My darling – having some very hot weather at the moment; everyone is getting very brown. I hope that you had good weather for your holiday at 'Viewlands.' By the way, I have heard that the portraits I told you about got home in March. The artist was Ley Kenyon. Anyway, I have sent you a photograph of the one of me. You should have it by now. Did you get the plans for that house? Cheerio darling. All my love. Arthur xx.'

Ley Kenyon's portrait of Arthur Garwell.

Flight Lieutenant Ley Kenyon DFC, tall, well-spoken, and with strikingly aquiline features, had employed his considerable artistic talents to forge travel and identity documents for the escapers. He was one of the ticketholders selected for the escape but, luckily for him, never got further away than Hut 104. During the many months of tunnel digging, he was asked to create a detailed pictorial record of escape activities. The only way to do it was to go to the tunnel face and see it for himself. He managed to capture the ingenuity and self-sacrifice of the enterprise in a series of vividly descriptive pencil drawings. Hidden at the camp, they were discovered after the war, returned to him, and went on to illustrate some of the many books that were eventually written about the Great Escape. He drew my dad as well, capturing his young face, his wavy hair, his piercing eyes, and his slightly bent nose with unerring accuracy. When I look at a copy of the drawing now and see him framed by the upturned collar of his RAF uniform, he looks so young – and so cool.

It was now the month of June, and the searingly hot summer weather continued. On June 3rd, he wrote:

> 'Darling – many thanks for your letter of March 3rd, which reached me this morning, taking just three months on the trip. I was surprised at the very long hours you have to work. We certainly have a much lazier time here; up at 9.00, to bed at midnight! We have been playing some Victor Silvester records tonight & I have felt in the dancing mood all evening. How I wish I had those dainty feet of yours to tread on! And then perhaps a walk in the moonlight. Well, as Van Toen's father always writes, "it must end sometime!!" Very cheering, that! But true! Have had bags of sun lately. Started at 9 am this morning & had to put on my shirt at 2 pm to stop myself from bursting into flames.
>
> Ever yours, darling.
>
> Arthur.'

Three days after he wrote this, on 6th June 1944, massed Allied armies crossed the English Channel and landed on the beaches of Normandy. It was D-Day, the largest seaborne invasion in history and the beginning of the end of the war in Europe. The BBC's news bulletins were immediately picked up on the camp's clandestine radio receivers. At last, the assurances of Reginald Van Toen's father that *"It must end sometime"* seemed to be coming true. His bed-smashing, cuckoo-clock building son, along with thousands of fellow kriegies, were a big step nearer to liberation. The excitement was palpable, and Arthur was feeling it too:

25th June 1944

'Darling – I am afraid I have very little to tell you about in this letter, but I'm hoping that I will beat it back home anyway. What do you think? You will know anyway when you receive it! (I'm pretty bright tonight, don't you think?) Incoming mail seems to have ceased altogether as far as English mail is concerned anyway. However, we can put up with that, providing it doesn't go on too long. Time is drifting along very nicely, don't you think? Maybe you find that it goes more slowly with work to do each day and with something to mark the passage of time. You must get terribly impatient at times, poor dear; I must admit that I do too – particularly when the war starts moving and you think that you can see a little bit of England appearing through the mist!

The last letter of yours I received was March 24th. It's a pity they stopped then because I was hoping to hear about your holiday. I suppose you are getting in bags of tennis and swimming. I have been in the pool here several times, but you know I reckon I'm not cut out for water sports being so short of "bone-cover." I get cold pretty quickly, and even when I'm warm, I cope just as well as you'd expect someone who has never been in the water all his life and suddenly decides to go in for the first time at the age of ninety-five!!

I wish I could find words to tell you how much I love you and how I am looking forward to being with you again.

Ever yours, darling.

Arthur.'

He writes to his family with the same aching desire to be home:

> 'How I wish I was sitting on the train somewhere between Hexham and Corbridge and could look up and see the house on the hilltop. I can picture it very clearly now in my mind – though I find it difficult to imagine so much green all around. You know we haven't much green here – only the dirty dark green of pine trees.
>
> Well, I am hoping to be with you fairly soon now – maybe before all the roses have died off! I definitely expect to have Christmas with you anyway. Cheerio. Lots of love. Arthur.'

With the grinding day-to-day monotony of camp life, it was easy to tell Joan that nothing much happened at Stalag Luft 3, but that summer, the murder of the fifty still hung heavily in the air. The new camp Commandant, Oberst Werner Braune, was appalled at what had occurred and granted permission for the prisoners to build a stone memorial to their fallen comrades. My father helped to build it, as his letter to Joan of 25th July confirms:

> 'I have been fortunate enough to get several days outside the camp in a working party at our cemetery here. It makes a very fine change to be able to do a few days' work! I wonder if you get too much of it. You seem to work very long hours. I'm sure, though, darling, that it won't be for much longer now. I definitely expect to be married to you and to have forgotten all about this place by Christmas – this year.'

A few days later, he tells his parents the same thing:

> 'I have been fortunate enough to get outside recently for a few days on a working party at our cemetery. Been doing a bit of stone dressing and laying some too!'

The memorial still stands today in remembrance of fifty young men who never made it home.

CHAPTER 22

The Dark Continent

By that August, Allied armies had fought, kilometre by hard-won kilometre, across the patchwork fields, hedgerows, and villages of northern France to reach, and then liberate, Paris. At the same time, a much bigger and bloodier battle was raging to the east as Russian forces advanced on their German enemies; the two brutal, opposing ideologies of Stalin and Hitler inflicting barely imaginable horrors of suffering and death on millions of helpless civilians.

Compared with this carnage, life in Stalag Luft 3, with its theatre productions, film shows, sports events, and vegetable growing, was a relative haven of tranquillity. Often boring, frustrating, and tedious, but safe - for those willing to stay put and see it out. Now the end was in sight. Now Arthur's perennial hope of being home before Christmas finally seemed to be within touching distance.

Joan darling – what can I tell you in this letter? I haven't the faintest idea of what to say or where to start! Life goes on here much the same as it has done for the last two years. The weather has been good, but we expect that at this time of year. I was just thinking; we shall soon have known each other for three years, and for two and a half, we have been apart – not fair, is it, darling? To me, it seems very much longer. Well, I feel confident that this black period is rapidly drawing to a close, though, of course, it may drag on much longer than we expect. I shall be very disappointed if I am here at Christmas. I wonder what fate has in store for us. It could be so marvellous or just the opposite. Have you had any more photographs taken recently? I should welcome another snap or two. I suppose it's very difficult to get photographic materials. I haven't had any more taken here recently, but I may get into a group in the near future.

Well, I told you I hadn't much to say. Oh yes, I forgot, I saw a good show the other night, 'Blithe Spirit' by Noel Coward. Reminded me very much of some of Thorne Smith's books.

Well, must say cheerio, dearest. I hope I'm with you soon. I love you. Arthur xx.'

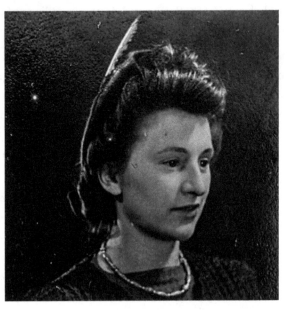

One of the many photos Joan sent to Arthur.

The next letter to his family is similarly upbeat:

'Dear Family – I haven't received any letters from you for two months. This morning I received Nora's letter of April 1st and was glad to hear that you are all well and getting along nicely. Nora seems to be doing very well at school and liking it too. I have had three letters from Joan this month, and she tells me that she has had a very pleasant holiday with you. I am so glad. I'm expecting to be up there myself pretty soon – almost as soon as this letter, I hope. I am keeping very fit, happy, and optimistic, as you will have already gathered.

The garden is going very well and showing signs of producing a big crop of tomatoes. I have just gathered in the French beans tonight. The quality is excellent, but the quantity is a shade short.

Well, don't forget I shall be dropping in to see you soon, so don't forget to keep the larder full.

Cheerio.

Love Arthur.'

Every chance Joan Shepherd had to escape the long hours of office work at Briggs Motor Bodies was taken to make the 140-mile journey north from Doncaster to stay with Arthur's family at 'Viewlands.' She loved her time there and was welcomed with open arms. Now coming up to 24 years of age, she was especially fond of 12-year-old Nora, maybe remembering the little sister she lost as a child.

The sweeping hills of Northumberland were a far cry from the bustling streets of industrial Doncaster; the haunting call of lapwings and the whisper of wind in the treetops a calming contrast to the incessant thump of giant metal presses. There were morning walks to the farm down the lane to fill a can with creamy fresh milk, still warm. There were strolls down to the little stone bridge over the rushing waters of Birkey Burn and on into the dark, secret woods beyond. There were the drifting scents of roses in the garden and baking in the kitchen. It was another world.

'My own darling – Unfortunately, I haven't received any more of your letters since last I wrote to you – I received Nora's April 1st letter this morning – the one in which she told me how you made an April fool of Dad. I had a very good laugh at it. I am glad that you two get on so well together. She's a very likeable little girl. You know I feel terribly out of touch with everything at home. I have noticed a terrific change in Nora's letters in two years. I'm sure I shan't know her when I do get back. Talking of getting back, darling, I'm sure it won't be too long now. Definitely before Christmas at the latest. What a marvellous Christmas that will be! You know, I'm very sentimental about some things, Christmas being one of them.

I hope, Darling, that you haven't been worrying about me too much recently. Always remember that I am being very patient and ever looking forward to that golden day when we shall be together again when I hope I shall be able to make you really happy for a change – instead of always being an infernal nuisance. Ever since I have known you, I have always been dashing off to catch a train or a plane. And then I get shot down and have to make love to you at a range of about seven hundred miles!! I'm sure you must think me a dead loss as a fiancé. Well, my dear, I hope that you, too, are being patient and not getting too fed up with your stuffy office. I myself am very fit and well. Still pottering around the garden and dreaming of that little home we shall soon have, and of all the things I shall grow in the garden! Well, if I don't beat the last letter home, I expect to get *back to you before this one!*

All my love to you, darling.

Arthur xx.'

Every kriegie was thinking about the future, how they wanted the rest of their lives to be when the war was finally over. For Joan's brother, Peter, it was already over, and she was worried about his state of mind as he struggled to recover from the devastating injuries he'd received in Malaya. Arthur tried to reassure her:

'You sounded worried about Peter in one of your letters. I'm sure he will be fine when he has settled down in his civilian occupation. You know it is a very big change to go from service life into an office. Most people here are keen to get away from what seems too artificial a life - farming seems to be the most popular idea of post-war occupation. I must admit that I have often thought of it myself. In my saner moments, I think that I already have something good in the Customs.'

By that September, there was another, very different, possibility still playing on his mind. One of Arthur's mates in Hut 109 was Flying Officer R. R. Michell, who hailed from the town of Salisbury in what was then the British colony of Rhodesia - now Harare, the capital of Zimbabwe. Both of them had piloted Lancasters for 44 (Rhodesia) Squadron based at Waddington. Both of them had been shot down over Germany and crash-landed their aircraft; Garwell in April 1942 and Michell eight months later, in December. Both had lost crew in the process; they had a lot in common.

In September 1944, Arthur wrote this to Joan:

'I have a strong feeling that it would be a very good thing to go abroad. I think I told you of it in one of my letters - and I wonder

what you think about it, dear? One of my roommates, Michell, a Rhodesian, may have the opportunity of taking over a pretty good wine and spirit business in South Africa after the war, and if he does, he would like me to go in with him. I often toy with the idea. You see, I sometimes feel that the Civil Service may prove a little red-tapish and slow and would tend to make one too 'deadbeat.'

It is hardly surprising that the thought of settling down into a life of plodding ordinariness held little appeal to men who had lived on the very edge of existence for so long, but Arthur knew that others might find his idea difficult to accept.

'To go abroad would mean the breaking of ties and separation from friends and relations, etc. For me, that would be perhaps a little easier than for you, as I have been away from home so long - though I still get very homesick at times, but I'm sure that if I had you with me, that would not be so bad. It would be heaven even if we had to live at the North pole! You know, I hope you realise how much I am in love with you, young lady! If I'm here much longer, I will have to start calling you old lady - and you can call me old man!! You know I have another birthday creeping up at an alarming rate.'

He was coming up to twenty-four years old.

'Oh yes, about this South Africa business. It's all very much up in the air and will be so probably for some months after the war. I shouldn't mention it in your letters home as they are sure to think I am quite mad and preparing to creep off one boat and dash onto another immediately bound for the Dark Continent! I shall probably end up anyway as a rather deadbeat, red-nosed Customs officer wearing a battered bowler & pin-striped pants - with a most charming little wife.

Darling, I love you so. Please keep yourself happy. I shall be back soon.

Ever yours. Arthur.'

I wonder now just how Joan felt about his idea of a new life in Africa. Given that much of her young life had seemed rootless, adrift, her yearning would likely have been for nothing more than love and stability. *'A most charming little wife'* might jar to modern ears, uncomfortable with such an old-fashioned stereotype, but Joan wouldn't have minded at all. She just wanted her man back, unscathed.

One thing I do know; Africa never quite relinquished its hold on his imagination.

CHAPTER 23

Waiting and Hoping

'27th September 1944.

Dear Family – Here's another month almost over, and I haven't much to tell you. Things are going along pretty smoothly. Summer seems to be changing very rapidly into another winter; we have already had a few slight touches of frost. I find that I am settling down to our main winter occupation – reading. I may do a little study, though it is fairly difficult at this stage when the war seems to be nearing its end.'

With news just surfacing that the Belgian cities of Brussels and Antwerp had been liberated, it was easy for the men of Stalag Luft 3 to see which way the tide was running, but Hitler was not done yet. In a desperate effort to reverse matters, the Nazis launched the world's first long-range ballistic missile; a revolutionary terror weapon dubbed the V2. It was a space rocket, pre-programmed to hit its chosen target with, it was hoped, devastating accuracy. Impossible to intercept, it arrived at almost 2,000 miles per hour, silently and without warning. There was no time to run for shelter. In the months that followed, thousands of them rained down on Allied cities, spreading death and destruction. The Nazis called it their 'retribution weapon.'

In total contrast, one of the main problems for the thousands of men confined by the high fences, barbed wire, and guard towers of Stalag Luft 3 continued to be boredom.

'My darling, I simply have no idea what I can write about tonight. I have received just three letters this month as against 23 last month. However, variety is the spice of life, or so they say. All three were from you, darling. You write remarkably fine letters, never dull and dreary as I'm sure mine often are. I have just been reading through some old letters of yours. I came across a sentence one which made me laugh. It ran, "I received a letter from you this morning about salted herrings."!! Poor dear, you must have found that one most uninteresting. The trouble is, you know that I sit down and write to you, and then time goes by, and I find myself writing again, and nothing has happened in between except that a few days or weeks have gone by. Oh, for the day, darling, when we shall be together again! Thinking back, I have a feeling I've said that before.'

Anticipation of their future life together was running high, but later in this same letter, there are a few innocent words that would come to shape that future in a way Arthur could not possibly have imagined.

'It was very pleasant to hear that you had a good holiday up at 'Viewlands' during the summer, but I was sorry to hear that you have since been ill. What was the trouble? I suspect that you probably caught the flu again. You must be more careful in the wintertime, darling.'

But it wasn't influenza; it was more serious than that.

As the year drew toward its close and with winter fast approaching, Arthur's earlier promises of being back home for Christmas began to evaporate. It would be his third in Stalag Luft 3.

'Darling, I hope you won't be too disappointed if I am not back for Christmas. I shall be thinking and dreaming of you particularly *then. Remember, take care, and don't go catching more flu! I love you always, darling. Ever yours. Arthur.'*

At the end of November, he tells his family:

'Everything is going along pretty well here. The weather, which has been pretty wet, seems to have cleared up, and last night, we had about 12 degrees of frost. Today the sun has been shining very pleasantly. Preparations are already underway for the construction of a skating rink, but I suppose the winter will prove too changeable to give us much skating. At the moment, I am busy cooking again. Two of us do it for three months at a stretch. When not cooking, we do other duties around the place - washing up, peeling potatoes, etc. In fact, by the time I leave here, I should be highly skilled in the art of housekeeping! Well, I'm afraid I shall disappoint you again this Christmas. I shall be thinking of you all then and no doubt trying to picture you sitting around the cosy fire listening to a carol service. Well, here's hoping for a reunion very early in the new year. I trust that you are all keeping very fit, well, and optimistic. Love, Arthur.'

His next letter to Joan is full of both optimism and desire:

'9th December 1944

My Darling,

What a wizard month this has been! I have so far received five of your letters and three from home. Thank you very much and especially thanks for the photograph – the one with the big eyes! You look very, very fit and extremely attractive. Your expression is rather as I imagine it was when you heard of the invasion on June 6th or as it will be when you hear of the armistice on…. I wonder when? I had rather given up hope of receiving more photographs, and I can assure you that this one came as a delightful surprise. I'm glad you got the group photograph I sent — the one with the feet. It is strange how many different opinions I have received about it. You think it is not so bad, my mother thinks it is marvellous — yet she dislikes the portrait — and Johnny's fiancée thinks I look seriously ill in it!!!

I'm glad that your tennis is going well and that you have managed to get on the works team. You must be pretty good at the game! I am at the moment very busy learning Afrikaans — just in case that opportunity to go out there materialises. The business, by the way, is situated in George, a town of 10-20,000 population lying somewhere on the East Coast, south of Rhodesia. It is, I believe, one of the prettiest parts of South Africa. I'm having great fun learning Afrikaans. It is a pretty easy tongue — rather like simplified Dutch. The most difficult thing is pronunciation — it is full of g's which are pronounced like the Scotch "ch" in loch. After a late lesson one evening, I spent the whole night dreaming about long words which I couldn't pronounce.

By the way, did I ever tell you of a dream I had in which we were married and had a little boy who was walking — age probably about 3 — and had red hair!! I wonder if it will come true?

Ever yours, darling

Arthur.'

I, of course, know the answer to that. It did.

Shortly after this letter passed the scrutiny of censor number 63 and headed for England, the Allied advance in Belgium suddenly ground to a halt. Hitler had launched a massive, surprise counter-offensive in a last-ditch attempt to gain the upper hand. Upward of half a million Nazi troops, supported by fifteen hundred tanks, poured across the hills and forests of the Belgian Ardennes and pitched, headlong, into the opposing American armies. With heavy snowfall and low cloud keeping Allied aircraft on the ground, the balance of power rapidly tilted in favour of the Germans – so much so that the American armies were forced into a series of costly retreats. The Battle of the Bulge, as it came to be called, was the bloodiest conflict on the Western Front in World War II. Tens of thousands of men on both sides were killed or injured before Hitler's armies were overwhelmed and forced to retreat in the following January.

It was still raging as, three days before Christmas, prisoner 117 picked up a pencil to write this, the last letter Joan would ever receive from Stalag Luft 3:

'My darling,

These continual Christmases are, I suspect, beginning to make me look a little foolish. Twice already, I've said, "Well, that's the last in here!" yet, Good Lord, here's another!! Darling, how I wish we could have been together. We must make the first one we spend together a four-in-one, extra special celebration. I wonder how you picture a Christmas here inside the wire? You probably think it is much worse than it really is. This year we have seven American Christmas parcels plus three normal American parcels. The Christmas parcels are really splendid, containing, among other delicacies, turkey, Christmas pudding, honey, ham, Vienna sausages, dates, sweets, etc. We have a cake made by an American ex-pastry specialist who is in the room, which has been maturing for a couple of months. In fact, I have no doubt that we shall have more than we can eat comfortably on Christmas day. There will also be a big show at the theatre and probably some sort of skating gala. The weather, by the way, has been splendid, very cold and hard, but bright and healthy. It really looks as if we will get plenty of skating this year. I shall probably have to make some sort of an effort to learn to skate!'

With unusually plentiful food to eat, theatre shows, and a skating gala, Christmas 1944 in Stalag Luft 3 stood in stark contrast to the vicious fighting going on outside. The letter continues:

'I have received seven letters from you this month, ranging from September 26th to November 3rd. I was very glad to get them and to hear the good news that you were well again. You know I was getting worried about you.

The two photographs of you and Bee reached me safely. I like them very much. It's a great thrill to see you again, darling. Well, here's hoping all your dreams come true very early in the New Year. I am ever yours, Arthur.'

Joan and Bee

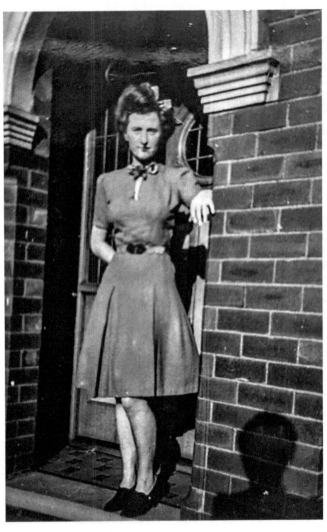

Another of the photos Joan sent to
Arthur wishing him a happy New Year.

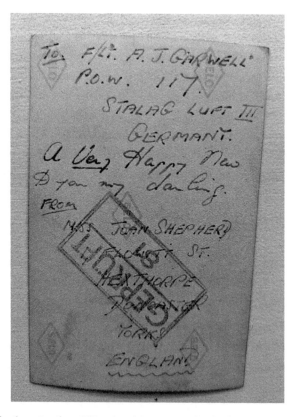

Joan had arrived at 'Viewlands' two weeks before Arthur wrote this letter, and she, too, was getting into the spirit of Christmas as well as dreaming of their future together:

'It's a week now since I came to stay at 'Viewlands' for the duration, and I can't tell you how much happier and content I've been in this gay little house on the hill. Family life is a wonderful thing, and it's the first real taste I've had of it since I was nine years old, and Christmas is almost here too.

Nora and I were out seeking holly this afternoon, and Mummy & I made mincemeat last night. Yes, and I'm learning to cook too. I've cooked the dinner for three days now, mind you mustn't expect wonders when we start in our first home together, but won't it be fun when we first really start to be Mr & Mrs, that is if you promise not to laugh when I make mistakes. You know I think we'll be the happiest and most disgustingly & obviously in love Mr & Mrs there ever was. I'm sure I shall kiss you in public, and without feeling the least embarrassed, that's when I get used to you, of course, cos I shall be terribly shy at first.

Look after yourself, my dear Arthur, because – yes, I know – I love you.'

As the end of the year approached, there was a strange mood in the camp - one of frustrated anticipation. Arthur had alluded to it in an earlier letter:

'We have reached a peculiar period in our life here at the moment - a sort of lull period in which we seem to have been waiting to resume our normal lives. It tends to make one very unsettled and restless.'

A little over a month later, the waiting stopped.

CHAPTER 24

A Postcard
from Lubeck

I remember when I first saw it, almost hidden among the letters
my mother had kept for all those years: a small, yellowing postcard
sent from Lubeck, Germany. Handwritten in hastily scribbled
pencil and dated Wednesday, 2nd May 1945, it read:

> *'Liberated at 12.00 o'clock today. I am very fit and well and feeling
> on top of the world! Hoping to be home within seven days. Just
> longing to see you again, darling. I will send a telegram when I reach
> England. Take care of yourself - be with you soon.*
>
> *All my love. Arthur.'*

It took some time for me to realise its exact significance to my
father's story. His last letter from the camp was sent in December
1944, and this was sent in the following May, five months later.
I had some sketchy knowledge of what became known as the
'Long March' but, up to that point, had little idea of what it was
like - and knew nothing about his part in it. To me, they were five
missing months.

These days it's easy to find out almost anything with an internet
search, but I wanted to know more about his personal experience,
and I'd never had the chance to ask him myself. I knew he'd
have endured it with his two roommates and close friends, John

Cordwell and Ken Carson, and so, when I managed to get in touch with their sons, Colin and John, I hoped they might know more than me. They did. A lot more.

So, with the help of personal accounts written by men who were there, I'll attempt to tell the story of the long march to liberation as experienced by the kriegies of room 7, Hut 109, and their fellow prisoners.

———

27th January 1945 was cold – bitterly cold. Outside room seven, heavy snow fell and froze; icicles hung like glistening blades from the eaves of the camp's long wooden huts. Beyond the high fence, the cooler, and the guard towers, the dark forest bowed beneath its heavy white canopy. The world shivered. Inside the room, ten men tried to warm themselves by the heavy iron stove. It wasn't easy.

The hope of approaching liberation was running high, but hope could be harder to deal with than disappointment – the prisoners of Stalag Luft 3 were wearily used to dealing with disappointment. They knew the Russians were coming, but when? They had watched the slow January days slide inexorably by and heard the distant thump of artillery shells grow ever closer. It couldn't be much longer, surely? But what then?

The answer, when it came, was sudden. Boots clattered on floors, doors were flung open, and guns waved frantically in shocked faces. Orders from the camp commandant – everybody had to leave. That night. On foot. After so many years of trying every conceivable way to get out, of tunnels, of ferrets, of successes and failures, now they were being ordered out – but there was no time to dwell on the irony of the situation; they had to act quickly.

What could they take? What must be left? How could they carry it? Clothes came first; what couldn't be worn couldn't be left – it was too bitterly cold to discard anything that might offer even a little warmth. Then food – always hungry, they grabbed everything edible and hurriedly ate what couldn't be carried. With a foot of snow on the ground outside, someone suggested they should build a sledge. The table in the middle of the room was soon flipped upside-down, and a bunk dismantled to fashion some makeshift runners. Then Room 7, Hut 109, was systematically smashed up in a search for nails to hold the whole thing together. With any damage to the huts normally resulting in charge of sabotage, it must have been deeply satisfying to inflict such wanton destruction with complete impunity. Finally, bed sheets and blankets were fashioned into a harness and the sledge loaded up with spare blankets, clothing, and food. With a last look around the tediously familiar walls that had imprisoned them for so long, ten roommates, ten friends, waited for the order to march into the night.

Getting 10,000 kriegies out of the camp was no easy task. The Americans from the South Compound went first, starting just after 9 pm. With food rations already severely limited, each man was handed a Red Cross parcel as they filed out into the night. It was well past midnight when Ken Carson, John Cordwell, Ginger Garwell, Mitch Michell, Reginald Van Toen and the rest of them manhandled their cumbersome, cobbled together, overloaded creation through the open gates, past the last guard tower, and out onto the snow-bound road to nowhere. No one, not even the German guards, knew their destination. All they knew was the general direction of travel - westward - away from the guns of the vast, vengeful Russian army, just 20 kilometres to the east. As they took one final glance back at Stalag Luft 3, they saw vivid orange flames licking into the blackness. One of the huts had been torched in a final, fitting, gesture of defiance.

A journey that started with high excitement, almost euphoria, very soon turned into a slow, trudging ordeal. Heads bowed against the driving snow, they looked like bedraggled polar explorers manhandling a sledge across frozen Arctic wastelands; two in the harness, pulling; two at the sides, steadying, and two more at the back pushing. Progress was painfully slow. Snow clung to eyebrows, sweat dripped, then turned to ice, boots struggled for grip, and toes began to freeze. Hour by endless hour, the ragged procession of prisoners, thousands of them, stumbled through the pitch-black night. Cold seeped relentlessly through layers of wet clothing, chilling aching limbs, making each footstep harder than the last. Vision narrowed to a single point somewhere on the back of the man in front. To fall back, to stop, risked slumping into a ditch and dying of exposure alone.

As dawn began to break, and with seventeen slow, painful kilometres behind them, a small town appeared ahead. Frozen, sleep deprived, and hungry, they hoped for some rest, but the Luftwaffe guards ordered them on towards the next town, eleven kilometres ahead. In the morning light, they could make out all kinds of discarded baggage littering the snow-covered verges, abandoned by weighed-down kriegies ahead of them. The men of room seven struggled on, pushing and pulling their heavily laden sledge, reluctant to throw anything overboard that might be needed later. In amongst the long procession of prisoners were terrified German families, the old and the young, fleeing westward with all the worldly goods they could carry. They knew what their fate would be if the Russians caught them.

By midday, after twelve hours of walking, the exhausted kriegies reached the next small town and stopped, hoping again for a chance to rest and eat, but, after a short break, they were forced at gunpoint to continue. Nowhere could be found to shelter so many men, and it began to feel like the ordeal would never end. The bitter cold was unrelenting. Some men fell by the wayside, too sick, frozen, and physically spent to continue, and, at some point, John Cordwell, too, gave up. He staggered away from the road and slumped into a huge snowdrift. I only know this because his son, Colin, told me the story when we first made our online connection across the Atlantic. This is what he wrote:

'The snow, cold, and wind were so bad that many POWs succumbed. My father was one of them. "I saw a snowdrift with my name on it. I staggered over and fell into it and immediately started losing consciousness. There was a brief moment when I realized that if I go to sleep, I'll never wake up. It was about then that I felt a sharp blow in my ribs as if I'd been run over by a lorry. I came to and felt a mixture of pain and rage!" He heard your father's voice saying, "Get up, you bugger, you're not dying here!" Your dad pulled my dad to his feet, and they continued the march.'

As much as they could, the kriegies looked out for each other, but some of them were beyond help.

It was night-time again when the ghostly white, frost-encrusted procession reached the village of Lipna. They had walked, shuffled, and limped a barely imaginable thirty-four kilometres since leaving Sagan the night before. The young Australian fighter pilot, Ken Carson, would later describe what happened next:

> 'Everything we had, all our food and water, was frozen stiff. That night we stood in a long column on the road, waiting to get into a barn for shelter. The temperature was twenty or twenty-three degrees below zero, and several chaps passed out in the cold. Even some of the guards were carted in with frostbite and frozen feet. We eventually got into a big barn and found some straw to sleep on. The barn was a mass of seething bodies, but it was good shelter.'

It was hard to sleep and even harder to scrape together something to eat from the deep-frozen provisions the men had managed to carry with them, but eventually, the long night passed. At 8 am the next morning, it was back on the road and out into the unrelenting snow and ice. Boots taken off during the night were frozen rigid. Putting them back on and trying to walk was agony. At midday, they reached a small town and were allowed to stop to try and get some food down. With their own supplies still frozen solid and with nothing provided by their captors, many resorted to bartering with the locals. They met very little hostility. With everything descending into chaos for both the prisoners and the German population, it seemed that a sense of compassion and common humanity was beginning to emerge.

After thirty minutes or so, they were back on the road. The Luftwaffe guards, many of them no longer young men, were just as exhausted as the kriegies. Some jettisoned their heavy weapons, unable to carry them any further. It would have been easy to escape, but there was nowhere to go, and it was much safer to stick together. As the afternoon light slowly faded into dusk, and with another thirty kilometres behind them, they came to a small medieval riverside town called Muscau. It was unprepared for the sudden arrival of thousands of men, all with an overwhelming need for somewhere to rest and something, anything, to eat. As the guards spread out to see what could be found, the prisoners stood and waited. Any warmth generated from marching soon leaked through damp clothing and out into the bitter night air. Teeth chattered as young, battle-hardened men shivered uncontrollably.

After what seemed like an endless wait, the marchers were split into large groups and sent to wherever rudimentary shelter could be found. The kriegies from room seven were herded into a huge barn-like building along with five hundred others. In peacetime, it served as a riding school belonging to a German nobleman; now, it served as a makeshift prison camp. As if cold, hunger, and exhaustion were not enough, there was something else to add to the misery - sickness and diarrhoea. Most of them were suffering from it. With no toilets and no privacy, any semblance of basic human dignity rapidly vanished.

Too weary to move, the next couple of days were spent in Muscau trying to rest and regroup for the journey ahead, wherever that might lead. The room seven lads decided to break up their repurposed table sledge and build five small sledges from the bits, hoping to make the coming trek a little easier. As they did so, the drip, drip, drip of melting snow signalled that conditions were changing - a thaw had set in.

It was 10 pm at night when they headed out into the darkness and started to march again, this time on slushy, rutted, hilly roads.

Over fifty men had been left behind, too ill to travel. Ken Carson's account takes up the story:

'A few kilometres outside Muscau, we decided that pulling the sledges without ice was stonkering us, so we jettisoned them and resorted to packs. At this point, hundreds of kriegies made the same decision, and the road was littered with sledges of all shapes, sizes, and designs, and also a lot of abandoned kit. We were determined to carry our food at all costs as we were not getting any rations from the Germans and did not know when we would get any. I made a haversack out of two towels and a bag to hang in front made out of an old shirt. At this point, I jettisoned one of my blankets and some old tools we had stolen on the way. Incidentally, all kriegies are expert thieves, and we stole when and where we could. In fact, we were a most unscrupulous crowd. We had to be.'

They plodded wearily on for hour after hour, almost in silence, each man lost in his own thoughts, driven on by the will to survive. Every now and then, they came to a cluster of roadside houses, and, just occasionally, a kindly inhabitant took pity on them and offered some water or a warm drink - if the guards weren't looking. Ken's account continues:

'We found lumping the packs mighty tiresome, as food, which we concentrated on, is very heavy. This part of the trip was rather cold and wet and, after marching all night, we arrived at a small village. We staggered into a barn and hit the hay rather willingly. Unfortunately, we had neither the time nor the energy to cook any meals, we were so knocked up. We had been five months on very short rations.'

The next morning a long line of bedraggled, unshaven, worn-out kriegies tramped the last few kilometres to a town called

Spremberg. They didn't know it, but their march through one of Germany's coldest winters was over. They had covered one hundred kilometres.

CHAPTER 25

Into the Unknown

It was now 2nd February. At 2 pm, the disheveled column of men was herded into an empty barracks where, at last, they had access to some warm food and water. It seemed like an unimaginable luxury, but not for long. Later that afternoon, they were marched out, past the menacing grey hulks of swastika-festooned tanks and down to Spremberg's sprawling railway goods yard, three kilometres away. There, waiting in the gloom, they saw a long row of empty wooden cattle wagons. Any thoughts that a train journey might be more comfortable than a march quickly evaporated when heavily armed guards hustled them towards the open doors and ordered them to board, thirty or forty to a wagon. Without a platform, many exhausted kriegies, lacking enough strength, had to grab an outstretched hand and be hauled up by others. A few, too ill to even stand, had to be carried. It took time to get nearly two thousand prisoners aboard, but finally, the big, heavy doors were slid shut and locked from the outside with iron bolts. There was no light, no straw on the floor, no water, no toilets, and no escape. With a sudden jolt and the clanking of couplings, the train lurched forward, hesitated momentarily, then moved slowly out into the darkening night under a cloak of smoke and steam.

They could only guess what fate awaited them. Even now, no one knows quite why Hitler, with the war close to being lost, decided to empty the prison camps near the eastern front and move hundreds of thousands of POWs westward. Some think he intended to hold them as hostages, others that it was to prevent them from joining forces with the Russians, but no one can say for sure. Crammed into those railway wagons like cattle destined for slaughter, some of them feared they might meet the same end, either by summary execution like the fifty escapees or as victims of an attack by Allied aircraft. Wartime train travel was a perilous business.

With such a tangle of bodies in each wagon, there was little hope of getting any sleep. Some lay on the bare floorboards; others sat with their backs against the swaying walls and tried to doze. A few stood. As the long night wore on, conversation dwindled away until little more than the monotonous rhythm of the train, trundling slowly through the darkness, broke the silence. It was no intercity express. Eventually, slivers of light appeared through narrow cracks to herald the approaching dawn. It had been a torrid night for those still suffering from sickness and diarrhoea; all they had to use were empty Red Cross boxes.

At some point on 3rd February, the train came to a grinding halt at a remote siding somewhere in the middle of Germany. The men were briefly allowed out under close guard. Some got a little water. Others got none. Then it was back on board with the prospect of another long, miserable night ahead.

On the morning of the 4th, the train slowed to a crawl and stopped at a goods yard close to the city of Hanover. After a brief break, the monotonous journey continued for another one hundred kilometres until, in the late afternoon, they arrived at their final destination, a town called Tarmstedt, not far from the northern port city of Bremen. It had taken forty-four painfully slow hours to cover the five-hundred kilometres from Spremberg. By now, the kriegies had been told where they were going; to yet another POW camp. As they spilled out of the cattle wagons with the bits of battered luggage and remnants of food they still possessed, they could at last hope for somewhere more comfortable to rest up.

It took two hours to walk from Tarmstedt to the new camp. By the time the first men in the long column of disheveled kriegies arrived at the gates, it was dark and raining heavily. They were ordered to stop and wait. The Luftwaffe guards had gone, replaced by guards from the German Navy who began the slow process of checking small groups of men inside, one after another. That left almost two thousand men queued up on a muddy track around the perimeter fence in a line some half a mile long. They were cold, miserable, hungry, and soaked to the skin. All they could do was turn their backs to the wind-blown deluge and endure. As the hours passed, some men collapsed, no longer able to stand. They were carried to the front of the queue and allowed in. Ken Carson's account takes up the story:

> 'We eventually got into the camp at midnight (some waited until 4 am), and as there was just the bare room, we had a slice of bread and slept on the floor. The German Navy controlled the camp, as it was intended for Naval POWs, and discipline was not so strict. However, the camp was very old, and as there were no stoves, fuel, beds, or bedding, we were not too comfortable. We were very glad to have finished the trip.'

Before the men from Stalag Luft 3 arrived, the camp, called

Marlag-Milag Nord, had been emptied of the Allied Merchant Navy prisoners it previously held. Thinking that it was destined to house German troops, they had managed to smash the place up before leaving. There were broken windows, holes in roofs letting rain in, piles of rubbish, and a trail of general destruction, but at least Arthur, Ken, John, and the rest of the boys from room seven had survived the toughest journey of their young lives. And there was no more marching – for now.

A few days later, on 11th February, the notorious Allied attack on the German city of Dresden began, unleashing barely imaginable horror on its helpless inhabitants. In a period of three days, over 700 RAF Lancasters and 500 American B-17 bombers dropped thousands of tons of high explosives and incendiaries on its ancient, densely populated centre. The firestorm that followed destroyed some 12,000 homes and killed an estimated 25,000 men, women, and children, many of whom were German refugees fleeing westward, away from the approaching Russians. Most of the victims suffocated when the vast conflagration sucked all the oxygen out of the burning air they were trying to breathe. It exemplified the tragedy of warfare and would go on to haunt the reputation of Bomber Command for years to come.

CHAPTER 26

The End Game

There was much to do at the semi-derelict new camp: roofs to repair, broken windows to fix, plumbing to re-connect - anything that could make life a little more comfortable for the worn-out kriegies. Food was still a problem, but by mid-February, Red Cross parcels began to trickle through. And then it was March, bringing with it the added glimmer of optimism that comes with the blossoming of a new spring. The Third Reich was rapidly collapsing, its armies in retreat. British forces were advancing from the west, Russians from the east, and Americans from the south. It couldn't last much longer.

Somewhere, fighting alongside the rapidly advancing British forces, was Captain Ronald Curtis of the Guards Armoured Division - Arthur Garwell's brother-in-law. On 5th March, he penned a letter to Sarah and Arthur senior, his new wife's parents, at 'Viewlands.' I have it in front of me as I write. It starts like this:

'Dear Mum and Dad,

Thank you so much for your letter which reached me during the week. Glad to hear that you are both well. You have my very sincere sympathies on your more recent troubles with poor Joan. It seems so awfully unfair that you should have all this added to your many other wartime anxieties. As you say, however, the one consolation is in the hope that Joan will make a complete recovery and that that will coincide with the homecoming of Arthur.'

'*Your more recent troubles with poor Joan.*' Before reading this, I didn't know that my mother's lifelong struggle with chronic anxiety – nervous illness they called it back then – had started as far back as that. Childhood bereavement, workplace bullying, worry about Arthur, and the deep unease of living through a war – all these things had combined in a cocktail of emotions poisonous enough to damage the mental health of a sensitive young woman. Arthur had no idea. He thought she'd had influenza. His mother would have struggled to understand. She was a no-nonsense, no-fuss kind of woman. Tough.

There had been no letters from their son and no news of his fate for many weeks. Ron's letter continues:

> '*I'm constantly trying to find out any information on Arthur's whereabouts but cannot yet find anything concrete. Some reports say that Luft III has been evacuated. I only hope that they will be in our line of march and that I have the remarkable luck to have some hand in setting him free. That would certainly be a crowning moment in our family life, wouldn't it?*'

A sense of optimism pervades his letter:

> '*Isn't news magnificent? We're just racing towards our ultimate goal now – the end of the war in Europe – what a relief that will be when it's over. I don't think the Japs will last long after that – if as long! Conditions here now are most hectic. I wish you could see some of these places – you could see then that we're showing the Hun no mercy – absolutely NONE!*
>
> *Well, I think I must away and write to my wife now – I'll write to you again soon, and rest assured, I shall keep my eyes open for Arthur.*

Au revoir for now, dear people, and may God bless you - please take care of Bee for me.

All my love as always.

Ron.'

By the end of March, it was becoming obvious that a second prison camp exodus was in the offing. British tanks and ground troops were just forty kilometres away and rapidly closing in on Bremen. Rumours as to what might happen next rumbled around the camp, and with the possibility of another march looming, preparations got underway. No sledges were required this time, so kriegies channelled their ingenuity into fashioning wheeled carts and backpacks instead. Hopes of imminent liberation had to be put on hold.

The order to march came on 6th April - a Monday. Early on the following morning, thousands of Allied prisoners, escorted by their armed guards, filed out onto the open road once again, this time heading northeast, away from the threat of British tanks and artillery, both Navy and R.A.F. prisoners marching together. German forces were now like the losing player in a game of chess, in a hopeless position but still making the next move, unwilling to surrender. It was chaotic and dangerous. Allied aircraft dominated the skies, ready to attack anything that looked remotely like an enemy troop movement. This time the threat would come from bullets, not blizzards; some from trigger-happy guards, others from their own side. In Ken Carson's words:

'We marched in long columns during the day and were shepherded into a field at night. We were a "bolshy" crowd and made our own slow pace, hoping the British army would catch us up, but we only

saw the Air Force, which strafed the column with tragic results to some of the Navy chaps. The first night out, we camped in a wet field, and unfortunately, Bowker (whom Bill will know from the Squadron and who was in our room) was shot in the leg by one of the guards while we were trying to pinch some straw. The same bullet went through another chap, but they were not seriously hurt. The same guard had killed one of our men about a fortnight before, much to the disgust of some of the other German guards.'

Were the room seven men still together? I don't know for sure, but I'd be ready to bet that at least Ginger Garwell and John Cordwell, Laurel and Hardy, were. They'd have been somewhere in that throng of prisoners spread out in the fields at night, trying to grab a little sleep under starlit skies. They, too, would have been bartering whatever they had of value in exchange for food with friendly but frightened locals as the guards began to lose control of their charges. They'd have ducked into roadside ditches for shelter when RAF fighters mistakenly strafed the long line of marching men, unaware of who they were. They'd have known that some of their fellow marchers had been killed and some injured as a result.

By Saturday 15th April, the march had reached a town called Cranz on the banks of the mile-wide, slow-moving river Elbe, just outside the war-wrecked city of Hamburg. They had walked for another sixty-seven kilometres. There had been moments of quiet contemplation for some during the journey; snatched opportunities to wander at will in the gently rolling countryside, bathed in spring sunshine, filled with hope; fragments of time to notice the soft, green grass underfoot and feel the breath of a gentle April breeze on the face. And to notice birdsong instead of gunfire.

After a day of rest, the kriegies were taken across the river by two ferry boats – the Franz Schubert and the Mozart, named after the two great Austrian composers, both of whom represented the pinnacle of Germanic achievement. There they were, carrying a war-weary cargo of survivors in a conflict spawned by a fellow Austrian, Adolf Hitler, a man, by contrast, who plumbed the lowest depths of moral depravity. It was an improbable irony.

Having crossed the Elbe, the march continued north-eastward in a rag-tag procession of disheveled men and wheeled contraptions. According to Ken Carson:

> 'There were prams and carts of every conceivable shape and size. Some bought, some stolen. Wheelbarrows were also popular. We concentrated on food and blankets, and each needed cooking pots, etc., which dangled from the carts.'

The following days passed in an increasingly chaotic shambles of bartering, foraging, bunking up in barns, sleeping in the open, and petty theft.

After a week of walking, they reached the outskirts of Lubeck on the north coast of Germany, an elegant port city adorned with medieval, red-brick, gothic architecture and famous, in normal times, for the manufacture of marzipan. Only now, it was overflowing with refugees, suffering from food shortages, and plagued with typhus. It was not a good place to house thousands of prisoners, so they stayed put for five days while more suitable accommodation was found. Where they ended up was six miles away, at a large country estate at a place called Trenthorst. Owned by a wealthy German business tycoon who'd made a fortune from cigars, it was huge, as were the cavernous straw-filled barns where most of the men found shelter. The spring march from Tarmstedt was finally over. It had taken three weeks to walk two hundred kilometres. The kriegies set up camp and waited impatiently for liberation.

Most of the Luftwaffe guards had been called away to other duties. Many of them had struggled through with the kriegies for weeks, enduring many of the same hardships. Those that had treated their captives well were rewarded with what the kriegies called 'Good Goon Chips' in anticipation of when roles would be reversed. The Germans still didn't know the connotation of Goon but hoped the hand-written tickets might offer a little protection when the time came, as they knew it soon would.

By 30th April, the British army had almost reached the makeshift camp at Trenthorst. Arthur and his mates could hear the violent explosions and rapid gunfire drawing closer, and they could see the steady stream of retreating German troops filing dejectedly past. Meanwhile, in Berlin, the Russian Red Army was closing in on the Reich Chancellery building, Hitler's headquarters. Holed up in his bunker below, the Führer of Nazi Germany, the architect of the Holocaust, knew that this was the end. He put a gun to his head, pulled the trigger, and slumped forward in a deepening pool of blood. He was dead. Beside him, his wife of one day, Eva Braun, had bitten into a cyanide capsule and joined him in suicide. Their corpses, along with that of their pet dog, were dragged upstairs to the Chancellery gardens, dumped in a crater, doused in petrol, and burnt, in accordance with Hitler's final instructions.

On the morning of Wednesday 2nd May, the trickle of retreating German troops turned into a flood. Hundreds of them filed past the watching kriegies, many of them throwing their guns and grenades into Trenthorst's picturesque, tree-lined lake. Then, at 12 noon, a British armoured car tore down the approach road of the estate, screeched to a halt, and was swamped by a crowd of whooping, cheering, crying, delirious ex-prisoners of war. The few remaining guards were rounded up and taken prisoner by the gleeful kriegies. It was over. The inmates of Stalag Luft 3 were finally free men.

Somewhere in the ensuing melee, Arthur managed to write his postcard to Joan:

> 'Liberated at 12.00 o'clock today. I am very fit and well and feeling on top of the world!'

A day later, Arthur was in Lubeck, having his ex-prisoner of war identity card stamped and waiting to go home. Ken Carson, meanwhile, had teamed up with Mitch Michell. The two of them, too impatient to hang around, managed to snatch a German car and, flouting orders, drove over six hundred kilometres to Brussels in Belgium. On arrival, they hitched a lift to England in a Lancaster and were among the first to get back. Arthur's turn came soon enough. As he prepared to board a flight, he found enough time to write one final letter to Joan:

> 'Darling - Here I am on my way back anyway. We are hoping to leave here by air and may even be in England today. I am afraid we may be detained for a day or two at some reception camp, then I understand we have 28 days leave.
>
> I have been reading a few newspapers here and expect that you will be very worried about what you read there. You will be glad to hear that we ourselves have been reasonably treated and, for the last three

weeks anyway, very well fed.

You will have been very short of mail in the last six months. I'm awfully sorry, darling, but since leaving Sagan, we have only been able to send about two cards. I haven't heard from you since November last year. In a day or two, we shall be able to forget about this letter-writing business anyway - for a long time, I hope.

I'm terribly excited and awfully impatient to see you again, sweetheart. I'm terribly afraid that you may have been unwell since I heard from you. You must have had a very worrying time in the last few months. Must close now - expecting to leave at any moment.

Arthur.'

I'm trying to imagine his emotions on that flight home. Did he think back to the crash in his burning Lancaster at Augsburg and the death of his friends three long years before? Or maybe his escape from the camp and those days locked up in the cooler? Or was it the desperate cold of the march still fresh in his mind? Or nothing like that? Perhaps it was elation at being free - or just quiet anticipation of the future life that was about to unfold.

I'm trying to imagine, but I can't.

CHAPTER 27

Homecoming

On the evening of May 7th, the BBC interrupted its scheduled radio programmes to announce the unconditional surrender of German forces and the end of the war in Europe. The following day was to be a national holiday, VE day. The news, though not unexpected, was met with unbridled joy and unleashed a day of wild, uninhibited celebration across the country and beyond. From the smallest villages to the biggest cities, streets were decked with bunting, pubs stayed open late, people danced, and strangers embraced. Six years of suffering, fear, threat, and loss were finally over – for most.

Like so many other families, Arthur's mother and father were waiting at 'Viewlands,' desperate to welcome their only son home, but he had somewhere else to go first; Doncaster, where Joan was anxiously waiting for her man to return:

'I'm sure I shall kiss you in public, and without feeling the least embarrassed, that's when I get used to you, of course, cos I shall be terribly shy at first.'

He'd not received that letter, but her shyness after so long apart would have been no surprise. What must her embrace and those first few words have felt like after the endless waiting for this very moment? Just days before, he'd been a prisoner, long confined to male company; now, he was in the arms of a woman, like a scene from the movies. And if this story was a movie, the camera would linger on the reunited lovers, wrapped in each other's arms, and the soundtrack would swell to a romantic crescendo just before the final credits roll. And in the minds of the departing audience, the war hero and his girl would live happily ever after. But real life isn't like the movies.

Soon they were on a steam train heading north. In the welcoming comfort of upholstered seats, the bare boards of a lumbering cattle wagon were already fading into memory. Arriving in the vaulted, Victorian splendour of Newcastle station, they walked hand in hand across the gently curving platform and made for the connecting train to Hexham. Across the River Tyne and swerving westward, leaving the rows of terraced houses and the industrial margins of the city behind, the little train headed out into the spring-green countryside. Arthur was nearly home. Through Stocksfield, where Uncle Tommy and Aunty Betty Middleton's house sat high on the steeply wooded banks of the river, and then past Corbridge. Not much further to go:

'How I wish I was sitting on the train somewhere between Corbridge and Hexham and could look up and see the house on the hilltop. I can picture it very clearly now in my mind – though I find it difficult to imagine so much green all around.'

Suddenly there it was, still sat on the horizon – 'Viewlands' - exactly where he'd left it.

Stepping out onto the platform, the journey over, they made a striking couple; he in his blue, RAF officer's tunic and peaked hat, she in a pale cream coat with a nipped-in waist, wide lapels, and shoulder pads, the height of fashion. Curious heads turned to look. Just the short haul up Oakwood Bank and Arthur's long trek from Stalag Luft 3 was finally over.

Was he greeted by his mum and dad with tears of relief and an outpouring of emotion? Probably not. They were Garwells, and things were likely a little more reserved than that. It must have felt so strange to walk into the house and see the familiar walls, the rack of pipes by the fireplace, the bay window seat, and the garden. Nothing changed, but everything changed. A pot of tea, the best bone china set down on the dining room table, and homemade cakes. Welcome home, Son.

Family reunion. Photo taken in the garden at 'Viewlands.'

Lovers reunited.

The next few days saw Sarah setting about the task of trying to put some meat on the slender bones of her son. He was the centre of attention, and not just at 'Viewlands;' the return of a local hero was news in Hexham too. Very soon, an invitation to address a gathering of Hexham's Rotarians arrived. The story had all the ingredients needed to captivate an audience; the fatal daylight raid on Augsburg, life inside Stalag Luft 3, escape, recapture, tunnels, and the long march. It made the front page of the Hexham Courant.

And then it all went wrong. My mother put it this way: *"They'd got their son back, so they didn't want me anymore."* As a child, I believed it. Now I see it in a different light, tempered by the experiences of life. She'd been ill with anxiety - *'That dreadful trouble with poor Joan'* - as Ron Curtis had put it. Arthur didn't know, and anyway, he was in love. But it was with a girl he only knew through her letters, and they were love letters. He wanted to marry her straight away, of course, he did – why wouldn't he? She'd been a photograph on the wooden walls of his hut for so long; now, she was a living, breathing, beautiful reality. But his mum and dad were concerned. Better not to rush. Take time to adjust. Get to know her better. He wouldn't hear of it; wouldn't listen to their reasoning. There was, as my mum put it, *"An almighty row."* Just a month after his homecoming, he walked out of 'Viewlands,' taking her with him. They headed back to Doncaster and Blossom's little terraced house in Flowett Street and began planning their wedding.

On 14th June, less than six weeks after the liberation at Lubeck, Arthur and Joan got married. The wedding photographs show them smiling for the camera in front of the arched stone doorway of The Parish Church of Saint John the Evangelist in Balby, Doncaster, just down the road from Blossom's house in Hexthorpe. I'm looking at a photograph of them now. He's in his RAF uniform; she's in an immaculate suit, her feathered hat tipped to the right. He clasps her hand tightly in his, their fingers intertwined. His mother and father, their disapproval put to one side, stand to his right. Arthur senior looks proud; Sarah looks tired but manages a wan smile. Young Nora, holding her bridesmaid's bouquet, stands a little shyly next to her big brother. Joan's father, Albert, and her injured brother, Peter, are both there. Emmie, her aloof stepmother, stands a little apart, clasping her handbag tightly.

Pilot to prisoner, prisoner to husband. He was just one of thousands upon thousands of men and women emerging, blinking, from the chaos of war. Young lives, newly filled with hope and optimism, making plans, trying to piece together a normal life in a world still littered with bombed-out buildings. For Arthur and Joan, now Mr and Mrs Garwell, a journey into the unknown awaited.

For others, the start of a new life would have to wait. While Arthur and Joan made their plans, one German prisoner of war, by some strange irony, was tending the garden at 'Viewlands.' Camp 18, Featherstone Park, not far from Hexham, was one of the largest POW camps in Britain, with two hundred huts over four compounds housing thousands of German officers and orderlies. For them, the war was over, but not their captivity. Many prisoners were put on day release to work in the local community. Franz Frisch, a teacher before the war, was one of them. Arthur's mum, mindful of her own son's ordeal, treated him with nothing but kindness.

I remember the rockery and paths built by that German prisoner in the garden at 'Viewlands' from my childhood. They are still there today.

CHAPTER 28

Austerity

Britain was broke. The vast expenditure necessary to conduct six years of relentless warfare had left the economy in tatters. Great swathes of the country's housing stock lay in ruins. Food and fuel were in desperately short supply. The situation demanded a radical vision for the future and the political will to push it through, and that, the public decided, was a job for the Labour Party. The general election of July 1945 delivered Clement Attlee's party a landslide victory and brushed Winston Churchill and the Conservatives aside. The man who led the nation to wartime victory was not seen as the social reformer needed for peacetime. It was time for a change.

Change, too, for Arthur and his new wife, Joan. They set up their first home together by renting a small flat in Ilford, on the edge of the blitz-ravaged East End of London – a world away from the rural tranquility of Northumberland but altogether better than room seven, Hut 109. Dreams of a new life in South Africa faded, as Arthur expected they would:

> *I shall probably end up anyway as a rather deadbeat, red-nosed customs officer wearing a battered bowler & pin-striped pants.'*

Demobbed from the RAF, he re-joined H.M. Customs and Excise but, based in the investigation branch, avoided the boring, pin-striped customs officer stereotype. *"He was off chasing smugglers,"* my mother used to say. In London's murky post-war underbelly, and with almost everything rationed, there was plenty to keep him busy.

I would know almost nothing about those immediate post-war years were it not for a large white envelope with an Australian postmark that dropped through the letterbox a short while ago. It contained a bundle of photocopied letters, originally collected together by Ken Carson. They'd been sent to me by his son, John. Some were from Ken to his mother and sister. Others had been sent to him by fellow room seven kriegies shortly after the war. In today's world, they'd have been texts or emails, soon to be lost in a vast digital dustbin. Instead, these letters, in the handwriting of the men who penned them over seven decades ago, bring those times to life, and three of them were from my father.

Before returning to Australia, Flight Lieutenant Ken Carson borrowed a car and took off on a whistle-stop tour of Britain with Bill Fordyce, a fellow Aussie airman and ex-kriegie. There were overnight stops at Oxford, Doncaster, Newcastle, Edinburgh, and Glasgow before a return journey to London via Gretna Green, Carlisle, and Leeds. They discovered a country of rural springtime beauty nestled between centres of urban destruction, a world of ration books, shortages, and ruined buildings, but of cheerful optimism. It created a lasting impression.

In the following year, 1946, and safely back home in Australia, Ken Carson, now employed at a bank, did something that seems extraordinary today; something that speaks volumes to the lasting bond forged between many ex-kriegies - he sent food parcels to some of his room seven mates in the U.K. Food parcels! That's how bad it was in battered Britain, once the biggest colonial empire in the World. The letters of thanks he received in return paint a vivid picture of life in the immediate post-war years.

The first of the letters is dated 25th August 1946. It was sent from Stockton-on-Tees by Pilot Officer W.R. 'Bill' Sampson, a long-serving room seven prisoner. He'd parachuted out of his stricken aircraft in April 1942 somewhere near the French port of Cherbourg, so he was taken captive in the same month as Ginger Garwell. It starts:

'Dear Ken,

Thanks a lot for your letter of 5th April and also the parcel you sent - they both arrived within a few days of each other a few weeks ago. The contents of the parcel are very nice indeed, and young Brian has just got to the stage when he likes a "tasty bit" instead of just milk, so they will come in very useful indeed. He is now just over six months old and is growing like a mushroom…'

Born in February 1946, young Brian would have been conceived in June 1945, just a month after his father returned from captivity in Germany. He was an early starter in the post-war baby boom. The letter continues:

'I see you have started to work in the bank again - how is work going down with you? I expect that, like the rest of us, you will have found it easier than you imagined. I have got quite settled down to civvy street again, and we are very comfortable in our flat, although of course, it is not our ideal home - still, with the housing position as it is, we are very lucky to have got one at all.'

Working in the local housing department, Bill Sampson soon had first-hand experience of the post-war housing crisis:

'Our housing programme is coming along slowly due mostly to a shortage of materials - we have 338 permanent houses under construction with plans prepared for a further 368, so by the end of the year, we should have over 700 under construction.'

A year later, things had moved on; he'd relocated to Scotland and been appointed to the post of Housing Architect and Town Planning Officer for the town of Arbroath, where work was just getting underway to build 2,500 new homes. Despite the personal success, his letter to Ken, sent in February 1947, paints a bleak picture of the national situation:

'Conditions have worsened, if anything, of late, as you will no doubt have gathered from your news service. There was a complete breakdown in coal supplies a week ago, and the whole country is now very seriously rationed as regards the use of electricity, both for industry and domestic use. Conditions in the industry are chaotic - almost 2,000,000 unemployed and no signs of any improvement. Conditions have been aggravated by the very severe weather - the whole country has been in the grip of a snowstorm for the past two or three weeks, and quite a lot of roads are still impassable.'

Between January and March 1947, Britain experienced its worst winter in living memory. It snowed somewhere in the country for fifty-five days in succession. Up in Northumberland, the little lane that twisted its way down the hill from 'Viewlands' to Hexham was impassable. Young Nora set off to walk the two miles to school across frozen snow drifts so deep that they covered the hedges.

If that wasn't bad enough, the cricket was not going well either:

'I see our cricket team hasn't put up a very good show during their tour

of Australia - did you manage to get to the test match in Brisbane?'

Finally, he gets to the main point of his letter:

'Before drawing to a close, I would like to thank you very much indeed for the wonderful parcel you were good enough to send us. It arrived a couple of weeks ago, and I can assure you that it was very much appreciated by both of us. I am only sorry we can't return the compliment at present but probably at some future date, conditions will have relaxed sufficiently for us to do so.'

He signs off, not with Bill, but with his kriegie nickname - Sam, short for Sampson.

In February 1947, Ken received a similar letter of thanks from John Cordwell, sent from Eltham in South London:

'Dear Ken,

I am breaking W.T. (wireless transmission) *silence to send you the grateful thanks of Frankie - my wife & me. Your parcel has arrived at a very opportune moment. In addition to all the usual current difficulties as a result of the coal shortage, we are just about to set up a home for the first time, having recently tracked down a flat. Frankie tells me she is prompted at the sight of so much food to send you her thanks in a fashion which I think exceeds her bounden duty as a faithful wife!*

To be serious for a moment, if there is any way in which we can repay you for your kindness, we shall be only too glad to do so.'

John Cordwell had, not surprisingly, kept in touch with his best pal from Stalag Luft 3:

'Ginger has given me odd snatches of information from time to time as to your activities - the last being that you have now bought a Jeep.

I wondered too if you were resigned now to chewing gum?

Cricket is not spoken of now except in hushed voices in darkened tap rooms, where reminiscences of bygone days are retold in hollow tones. Tiddlywinks is to be adopted as our national sport.

Having reached home on 9th May 1945, I was married on 9th June 1945, so you see, my freedom was short-lived. I reverted to my former status and became a schoolboy again, and I am now reaching the end of my school days. Recently I passed my final examinations in architecture, and by Christmas, I hope to have done the same in town planning. Frank Knight - of 120 block, you may remember - is with me at school and should finish his town planning by Easter. Many RAF types are still clinging on like grim death, including Squadron Leader Willis Richards! Many others who had been demobbed are being asked to re-join for four years.

At the moment, I am engaged in preparing a scheme for an international exhibition to be held in London in 1951. With the heavy demands on labour and materials, it is difficult to imagine it being possible. Today things are about as good as they were in Germany. The electricity is cut, the gas is operating at low pressure, and anyone with coal is regarded with suspicion, but except for the inevitable "bod" with a grouse, people are quite cheerful since they feel that things can only get better from now onwards. This bad weather is indeed unfortunate since our production has leapt month-by-month in a most encouraging fashion.

Well, I must close now and press on with the exhibition, so once again, Ken, thank you from,

Sincerely yours,

Frankie and John Cordwell.'

Arthur and Joan received a similar parcel from Ken later in the same year.

'Dear Ken,

We received your parcel safely about a month ago. I would have written earlier to thank you, but we have been enjoying three weeks' holiday in Northumberland, and I couldn't get down to it. It was a most welcome parcel, and we really appreciate your kindness in sending it. The tinned bacon was a treat even though it reminds one of the old times. We have Joan's grandmother staying with us for a couple of weeks, and she has what you might term a "bacon tooth," so it arrived at a very convenient time. We feel, however, that you should give this parcel sending a rest for a year or two. We do pretty well, really, on the rations.

Things have been happening in the Garwell household since I wrote last. You will notice that we have left Ilford. We have quite a nice flat here, which we, fortunately, received in June.'

The new flat was above an arcade of shops called Electric Parade in George Lane, South Woodford. It was a little further away from the blitzed inner city of London and, even better, not far from the green expanses of Epping Forest. His sister, Beatrice, and her husband, Ron, moved into another flat in Electric Parade at about the same time. My mother had fond memories of the time she and her sister-in-law were able to spend together back then. Arthur's letter continues:

'It has been great fun setting up a home, with bags of fun for everyone - except the old bank balance, which has contracted a sickness from which I fear it will never recover!'

And then some news personal to me:

I don't know whether I mentioned this in an earlier letter, but we have an offspring on the way - due in January!

I can report that I arrived exactly on time. My mother gave birth at Wanstead Hospital, then a grand Victorian pile built in the elaborate Venetian gothic style. It was not an easy birth. *"You were born with a pointed head,"* she used to tell me. *"When the nurse brought you to me, I just cried and said, "He's beautiful."* Happily, the soft bones of her baby's skull assumed something approaching normality soon enough.

'This has been a wonderful summer for the weather anyway - right up to the best East German standard. The family was down here in August for a fortnight, and the old man and I went to the last test match with the South Africans. It was so hot that we had to clear off at teatime!

The harvest has been good, though it has not given the weight of grain expected. I think it suffered from the earlier dry weather. Economically, of course, we are in a frightful pickle, and with the basic petrol going off and cuts in tobacco and films, we look like having a pretty austere winter.

The loss of investments abroad during the two wars, coupled with the developments in industries elsewhere during the same period, seems to mean that we have to export one pound's worth of goods for every one pound's worth we import, and we have never done that at any period in our history (I believe).'

There are common themes in this post-war: ex-POWs, letters, new homes, new babies, careers, economic woes, and cricket. Dark memories of the war were still there, haunting like ghosts, but the excitement of starting to build lives that could only be dreamt of in Stalag Luft 3 was helping to push them aside.

For some, however, that was impossible. In July 1947, after a lengthy and complex investigation by the Royal Air Force Police Special Investigation Branch, eighteen members of the Gestapo were hunted down and brought to trial at the War Crimes Court in Hamburg, accused of murdering the fifty Stalag Luft 3 escapers. One man called to testify was none other than Friedrich Wilhelm von Lindeiner - the Stalag Luft 3 Commandant at the time of the escape. Now 68 years old, he'd been held prisoner by the

British for two years in the so-called 'London Cage,' a secretive establishment occupying three grand houses in leafy Kensington. It was run by MI19, the section of the War Office responsible for extracting information from enemy prisoners of war, often using brutal methods little short of torture. Von Lindeiner had been horrified by the execution of the fifty. When questioned at the hearing in Hamburg, he is said to have stated that he would rather have put a gun to his own head than have carried out such an order. Former prisoners at Stalag Luft 3 testified that von Lindeiner had always observed the Geneva Convention and had been respected by the senior officers in his charge. The trial ended in September. All the defendants were found guilty, and thirteen of them were sentenced to hang. Von Lindeiner was repatriated to Germany later that year, where he lived out the rest of his life in peace. He died in 1963, aged 82.

It was now 1948, three years after the war in Europe had ended, yet food parcels were still arriving from Australia:

'Dear Ken,

We received your food parcel a week or two ago. It was on the way for an awfully long time but was nonetheless made very welcome when it arrived. It was dealt with promptly and most efficiently! We are very grateful to you, Ken, for your kindness which we very much appreciate, and we three wish to say thank you very much once again.

Garwell junior is turning out a fine young chap. He now sports two wicked teeth which, given half a chance, he sinks with great gusto into your ear or nose or any part he can get hold of. He is now eight months and weighs about 19 pounds. I shall send you a few snaps shortly. We are having some prints made.'

According to my mother's often repeated story, those wicked teeth brought a painful end to her breastfeeding days.

> *'How is life treating you these days? Do you do any flying? I have a feeling that I may be roped back into some sort of reserve in the near future. Things are beginning to look anything but healthy.'*

The problem was Russia and the spread of communism across Eastern Europe after the war had finished. Bulgaria, Romania, Hungary, Poland, and eastern Germany had all come under Stalin's control, and the West felt threatened. Winston Churchill, with his typical talent for coining a catchy phrase, likened the dividing line across the continent to an 'Iron Curtain.' The name stuck. Arthur had an insider's take on the situation:

> *'We have had my wife's cousin, a Canadian girl, and her husband staying with us this week. They were both out in Moscow for a year, where he was, for a time, the British Consul. They gave us some interesting gen on conditions over there which are by all civilized standards incredibly bad. The standard accommodation in Moscow is apparently one room per family. They are far from recovered from the devastation of the war but still seem to have an enormous force under arms.'*

That may have been a concern, but things much closer to home mattered more:

> *'I'm hoping to get myself fixed in a nice country station soon. Up to now, you see, I have - and still am - an unattached officer of Customs & Excise. I, therefore, do relieving in and around the central London area. Now, however, I am of sufficient seniority to apply for a fixed station of my own, and I would very much like to get away from London and into the country. We would like to get a house of our*

*own, and I then hope to seriously challenge old Mitch in the family
stakes!'*

Then comes news of his old friend for whom things were not
working out quite so well:

*'We had Johnny Cordwell and his wife round here some time ago.
They are now back together again after having lived apart for some
months. He was not too happy about things then.*

*We go to Northumberland next week for my summer leave (three
weeks). Already, however, there's a nip in the air, and autumn is
beginning to establish itself.*

*The summer this year has been very poor (my tomatoes were not
nearly up to Luft III standards). Cricket was the most successful thing
of the summer. I saw part of the last test at the Oval. Your team was
really fine - much too good for us.*

All the very best to you,

Ginge.'

There was another birth in 1948 - one that would make
healthcare free to all, not just the wealthy. The National Health
Service, undoubtedly the crowning achievement of Clement
Atlee's Labour government, came into being on July 5th. Arthur
wouldn't have known it then, but Joan, his young wife, was about
to be taken into its care.

CHAPTER 29

Varying Fortunes

Arthur's last letter to Ken Carson in Australia, sent in December 1949, starts jauntily enough:

'Dear Ken,

I was most agreeably surprised to receive your letter and to know that you have not perished in the bush as I suspected but that you are, in fact, very much alive. May I at once offer my most sincere congratulations on your marriage and wish you and Lorna a life of happiness and prosperity together.

You might at least have made some attempt at satisfying my curiosity by sending a photograph of your wife. I doubt if you will be dropping around to see us for a year or two. I shall definitely expect one in your next letter.'

And then the tone changes:

'*Life for us has been one of varying fortune this past year. Joan, unfortunately, has been very ill with nervous trouble. She has twice been in hospital for long periods - the last from October until a fortnight ago - and is now on holiday recuperating.'*

So, his parent's fears were not unfounded. Maybe it was post-natal depression that triggered the final descent to a place so deep and dark that there seemed to be no way out. Or maybe it was the culmination of past events; the childhood trauma of losing her mother and little sister to tuberculosis; a father's rejection when her nursing career failed; the workplace bullying on the factory floor; the perceived rejection by Arthur's otherwise caring parents. Added to that toxic mix was the fear and uncertainty caused by six long years of war and the unrealistically high expectation of enjoying a 'happy ever after' marriage to a man she barely knew, except for his prison camp letters. It was only five years earlier that she had written:

> '*You know I think we'll be the happiest and most disgustingly & obviously in love Mr & Mrs there ever was.*'

The collision of hope with reality was stark.

Anxiety, depression, an inability to function normally – back then, it was called a nervous breakdown and carried with it a heavy stigma. There were no talking therapies, no understanding ears to listen or care, and no antidepressant drugs. It was all locked inside, a hidden disease.

And yet she was, despite her suffering, still a loving mother to her baby son, who, somewhere in the deep recesses of his memory, can recall her soft, gentle voice and the lullabies that sung him to sleep.

What happened to my mother during those two long periods in hospital would not happen today.

Electroconvulsive therapy, ECT for short, was a routine treatment for mental illness back then and was administered for almost everything, from schizophrenia through to severe anxiety and depression. It was brutal – literally shocking. Putting electrodes on each temple and passing a split-second surge of high-voltage electricity through a patient's brain induced violent bodily convulsions, which, for some reason that is still not fully understood, could sometimes alleviate symptoms. In the 1940s and early 1950s, anaesthetic was thought to be unnecessary as the sudden shock produced instant unconsciousness. The convulsions that ensued could be so violent that, on occasions, bones were fractured or dislocated. This was the treatment she endured during her first stay in hospital. It didn't work.

Two childhood memories are forever lodged in my consciousness: one was the name of a place, the Atkinson Morley Hospital, and the other was something my mother called a prefrontal leucotomy – better known now as a lobotomy. She spoke of them often.

Lobotomy was a simple procedure involving two 8cm metal spikes attached to wooden handles. Holes were drilled in each side of a patient's skull so that the spikes could be pushed into the soft brain matter. Once in place, they were swept from side to side, severing the connection between the frontal lobes and the rest of the brain. The whole procedure could be completed in little more than five minutes. In the late 1940s it was seen as some sort of miracle cure for severe mental illness, and the foremost practitioner in Britain was Sir Wylie McKissock, a renowned neurosurgeon based at the Atkinson Morley Hospital in the well-heeled London Borough of Wimbledon. And that's where Joan endured her second lengthy hospital stay. Such was McKissock's enthusiasm for lobotomy that he would routinely pack up his instruments and take off in his car at weekends to perform the procedure at smaller hospitals across the south of England. He would have pushed his long metal spikes into my mother's skull too.

The results of lobotomy were random; some patients improved, some stayed much the same, but many had their lives ruined, their mental capacity dulled to a shadow. It was the treatment used to deaden the wild impulses of McMurphy in Ken Kesey's novel 'One Flew Over the Cuckoo's Nest.' The procedure gradually fell from favour and was all but abandoned when drugs to treat mental illness came into use in the 1950s.

Joan was one of the luckier ones. Arthur certainly thought so, even though it was too early to know for sure. He writes:

'This time, there is no doubt that the treatment has done the trick.'

The next part of Dad's letter to Ken revealed something that I didn't know, and it came as quite a surprise:

'John, the laddo, has been staying with my people since October, and we haven't even seen him since then. We are going there to collect him in the middle of January. I don't suppose we shall know him after all this time. He will be two next month.'

I have not even the dimmest recollection of that three-month separation from my parents and, for some reason, was never told about it.

These troubles were not how it was meant to be for Arthur and Joan, but although their dreams of a happy post-war life were unravelling around them, there was still room for optimism:

'I don't think I have written to you since we moved to Epping - that is a year ago. We have a very nice little house - a bungalow, and with it half an acre of land. I now keep a few poultry, have a large vegetable garden, nice lawns (at least I hope they will be nice soon), and an orchard which I am now planting. Altogether it is a very pleasant

spot. Epping is a small town (population 5,000) about 15 miles from London. It is best known for its famous Epping Forest. Perhaps the best thing about this place is that I was fortunate enough to be able to rent it - at a controlled rent too. It is a particularly suitable spot for the boy.'

The pebble-dashed 1930s bungalow sat towards the bottom of Bower Hill, three-quarters of a mile down from Epping's busy high street. Its long back garden, shaded in places by tall trees, stretched as far as a small stream beyond which lay open fields, hedgerows, and the gently rising landscape of rural Essex. It wasn't quite the same as the house that John Cordwell had designed for Arthur in room seven, Hut 109, but it was close enough. The back door opened into a tiny kitchen equipped with little more than a pot sink, a wooden draining board, a gas cooker, and an old-fashioned, green-painted kitchen cabinet with frosted glass doors and an enamelled pull-out work surface. A pulley-operated clothes airer hung from the ceiling above the cooker. There was a separate pantry for storing what little food post-war rationing provided. A dining room and bedroom faced the long back garden, and on the other side of a narrow hallway, a sitting room with a bay window and a second bedroom looked out over the front garden with its neat, square rose bed. The bathroom, like the kitchen, was tiny.

As for the chickens, I can dimly remember childhood trips to the far end of the long garden to fetch freshly laid eggs from the coop. There is a photograph of my dad carrying me in his arms.

Anyway, as you see, I'm getting myself well dug in. The only fly in the ointment has been my wife's illness, and we pray that we have seen the last of that.

Memories of the long years in Stalag Luft 3, although slowly receding, were far from gone:

'Do you ever hear from Mitch these days? I haven't had a letter from him for at least a year. I believe it's his turn to write too. I haven't much news of the old boys from room seven. It was seven, wasn't it? You would think that travelling in and around London as I do, I would be sure to run into an ex- kriegie now and then. Cordwell, of course, I do see once in a while. I hear he is now in Nigeria working on some very large scheme for building a university and hospital. He has done very well with his firm and is now one of the junior partners.'

John Cordwell had come a long way since sketching house plans for his pal in the camp, but another part of his post-war life was in shreds:

'Unfortunately, however, his marriage has had it. He is hoping to get a divorce. The petition is due to come up any day now. He has been ill with nervous trouble, and most of it seems to have been due to incompatibility of temperament. His wife is a pretty tough specimen.'

He could survive a near-death experience when his plane crashed, endure years of privation in a prison camp, battle through the freezing cold of the long march, and emerge from it all with his mental health intact, but his marriage - that was a different matter. These young men were trained to meet the challenges of warfare, not relationships.

In the final paragraph of his last letter to Ken, Arthur harks back to their drunken, wire-climbing escapade of Christmas 1943:

'Here's Christmas again. Don't they come around quickly? I trust that on this occasion, now that you are a man with heavy responsibilities,

*you will behave with a little more propriety than you usually display
at this time of year!*

*I've been puzzling for some time to try to think of a suitable present
for you and your wife. Most things are liable to some sort of duty
complication. I have decided that the best way would be for me to
arrange for some periodical or other to be sent directly to you. I thought
you might like something to keep you in touch with affairs in this
old country at the moment. However, I can't think of anything that is
suitable, other than perhaps Picture Post. If something like that starts
rolling up, don't send it back!*

Wishing you both all the very best for Christmas and the New Year.

Yours sincerely.

Ginge.'

Arthur and Joan had now been married for four and a half years.
As the chimes of Big Ben rang out in the dying moments of 1949,
thoughts turned to the next decade. What would it bring?

CHAPTER 30

Through the Eyes of a Child

August 1950. It's early in the morning. My father takes me in his arms and sets off walking up the hill to Epping station. It doesn't take him long. As he strides up the steps of the concrete footbridge spanning the railway lines, I can see over the parapet to the tube train waiting below. To my infant eyes, it seems a terrifying drop, and a seed of acrophobia, a fear of heights, is planted in me, never to leave. He hurries to the London-bound platform, clasps my hand, and we step through the open doors of the nearest carriage.

We are not seated for long. As the train moves off, gathering speed, he looks at me and smiles. *"Come on, Son,"* he says, and, taking me in his arms again, he heads for the front of the carriage and opens the door at the end. There is a brief rush of wind and noise as the train's wheels clatter over the tracks below, and he steps through to the next carriage. The procedure is repeated until he reaches a door that I now realise would have displayed a warning in bold letters – 'No Entry.' In those days, the electric motor that powered a tube train was not slung underneath, hidden from view, but took up the whole of the carriage behind the driver's compartment. This is what he's brought me to see.

He turns the handle, pushes the door open, and steps into a narrow corridor. To one side, behind a clear screen, is the menacing mass of the huge motor. I hold him tightly, fascinated and frightened in equal measure by the noise, the smell, and the sense of danger. If I concentrate hard enough, I can see the scene now, over seventy years later. I think there were flashes of electricity, but maybe my memory deceives me.

He's on his way to work in the post-war sprawl of London, but I'm not going all the way with him. Theydon Bois, Debden, Loughton, Buckhurst Hill - the stations come and go until the snaking train squeals to a halt at Woodford. That's where he's taking me – to a day nursery.

Stashed away in my mother's carrier bag of memories, I found an old, yellowing postcard. Written on the back in my father's handwriting are these words:

'To my beloved and most courageous wife on her thirtieth birthday.

John says many happy returns, mummy.

Arthur & John. xxx'

The year 1950 is written at the top and underlined. It's in my mother's distinctive handwriting. I don't remember our separation when I was two and a half years old. I just remember the journey to the nursery with my father. His war was over, but her battle was not; she was in a hospital again. That's all I know. I don't know for how long or even where, but I do know that it was for the last time. Mental illness left an indelible mark, but it didn't break her. Their married life resumed.

What can I remember from my early childhood? I can remember his car; a black Wolseley 14-horsepower saloon with brown leather seats and those odd little illuminated arms called trafficators that popped up (or sometimes didn't) before a corner. I can even remember the registration number - PUR 998. I can remember standing at the end of our drive, looking up the road, waiting and waiting for him to arrive home from work. I can remember the front garden; the golden buddleia with its orangey-yellow spherical blooms that arched over the front porch; the red and pink flowers of the snapdragons that opened like jaws when I squeezed them.

And then there are the stories my mother told me; how he once avoided killing a child that ran out in front of his car but couldn't miss running over the child's foot, and how a deer jumped out of the trees in Epping Forest one dark night and landed on the Wolseley's bonnet. But for me, the best was the one about the day that he didn't arrive home from work because he'd missed the last underground train to leave London. It sums up something about him; he was a bit of a maverick. Most people would make sure that they didn't miss the last train home, and if by some chance they did, they might have found a hotel for the night. But not him. He set off to try and thumb a lift back home but ended up walking the full seventeen miles to Epping, much of it through the black expanses of Epping Forest. As dawn broke and he wearily trudged across the bridge that spans the railway line by Epping station, he glanced down only to see the first train of the morning pulling in. Even in his short-lived escape into the forests surrounding Stalag Luft 3, he hadn't managed to walk that far. What made him miss the train, I can only guess; maybe a late night after-work drinking session, or maybe not. It was his secret.

He joined his local cricket team, the Epping Foresters, and soon took on the role of captain, his slim build and athletic ability ideally suited to fast bowling. The club's pitch, on Bell Common, was sandwiched between the passing traffic of the A11 and the edge of the forest and, happily for my father, was ideally positioned for an after-match pint or two at The Spotted Dog pub on Ivy Chimneys Road. Many hours were spent at both locations.

A skipper once more - this time of Epping Foresters cricket club.

It should have been a happy infancy for Arthur and Joan's firstborn son, but one of the earliest and most indelible memories I have is of lying in my bed at night and hearing the raised voices of my parents arguing. No words, just voices; his was the louder, the more strident; hers the more defensive. Children shouldn't have to choose sides, but even at that young age, I chose hers. They wouldn't have known it, but their child's night terrors were spawned in those dark, lonely moments.

It was easier for them to be in love when they were separated by war and seven hundred miles, and when the yearning for a 'normal' life and a happy marriage spilled out onto the pages of their letters. The reality, of course, was very different. It always is. She was not the happy little 1950s housewife beaming with satisfaction in some advertisement for a television or a washing machine. And he wasn't the 1950s husband arriving home from the office in a pinstripe suit and a trilby, ready to pick up his pipe and slippers and settle down for the evening. How could they be? My father was better able to handle a burning Lancaster in its death throes than he was a wife struggling with her mental health.

But one of his dreams did come true; in the letter, he sent to Joan from his prison camp in December 1944, he wrote this:

'By the way, did I ever tell you of a dream I had in which we were married and had a little boy who was walking – age probably about 3 – and had red hair!! I wonder if it will come true?'

In August 1952, Joan gave birth to a baby boy. He had strawberry blond hair. They named him Timothy Peter, and, sure enough, by the age of three, he was ginger just like his dad. It wasn't just the hair, though; even at that tender age, there were clear signs that my younger brother had inherited some of his father's personality too. On his first day at the little Church of England school in the hamlet of Theydon Garnon, he decided to abscond, aged four. Slipping unnoticed from the playground, he set off to walk the one and a half miles home on his own. Past the Merry Fiddlers pub and the old farmhouse on the corner, past haystacks, hedges, fields, and streams, he ambled happily along the winding country lane, bathed in the sunshine of high summer. Meanwhile, back at the school, the discovery that one of their infant pupils had disappeared led to panic not entirely dissimilar to that induced in the guards at Stalag Luft 3 when Ginger Garwell and his delousing party cohort melted away into the forest. The level of his mother's shock when Timothy strolled down the drive to the back door was only matched by the level of her infant son's nonchalance. That mischievous, independent nature worried his mum but endeared him all the more to his dad. Later in life, my mother told me this: *"When your dad got home from work, he would often lift your brother onto his knee but send you to bed."* It hurt a bit when she told me, but I wasn't aware of his unconscious favouritism at the time.

There was one more addition to the Garwell family, but it wasn't another baby. Rustler, the Golden Retriever puppy, arrived unannounced one day, cradled in my father's arms – yet another redhead. The two of them formed an attachment that only seemed to strengthen when, sometime later, his canine buddy stole the Sunday joint from the kitchen when no one was looking, much to my mother's dismay. With a prisoner of war's memory of hunger pangs, it was an easy transgression for him to forgive – or maybe even admire.

My memories of those early years are fleeting: the sun-soaked summer Sundays spent on the village greens of rural Essex to the sound of bat on ball and occasional cries of *"howzat!"*; the long, boring hours sat with my little brother on the back seat of the Wolseley outside the Spotted Dog pub clutching a tomato juice and a packet of Smith's crisps (the ones with the twisted blue wrappers of do-it-yourself salt) that forever invalidated the meaning of 'just a minute'; a visit to the hospital after mistaking a bottle of paraffin left in the garden for fizzy pop; being plucked from the sea at Eastbourne after disappearing under the waves; and my first, but second hand, bike - the one my dad told me must have been scratched when Father Christmas brought it down the chimney.

As those years passed, my parents' marriage was slowly deteriorating, suffused with mutual dissatisfaction and disappointment. They tried to hide it, as so many couples did, but their wartime dreams were evaporating like mist in the morning sun.

CHAPTER 31

Doris and John

In 1951, an ageing Winston Churchill (the MP for Woodford) became Britain's Prime Minister for the second time after Labour lost the general election. In 1952 King George VI died, and in the following year, his daughter, the young Elizabeth Windsor, was crowned Queen. The spectacle at Westminster Abbey, with all its pomp and ceremony, was captured for a fascinated nation on flickering black and white television screens. Then, in the summer of 1954, food rationing in Britain finally stopped after fourteen long years of coupons and shortages. It was a hugely welcomed liberation.

In the following year, 1955, Arthur took Joan to see a newly released and soon to become famous film: 'The Dambusters.' One scene, shot inside the Officer's Mess at RAF Scampton, immediately grabbed his attention. He could easily recognise his old 83 Squadron base, but there was a new addition to the familiar surroundings; clearly visible on the wall of the crowded room was a large painting in a gilded frame. It was 'The Briefing' by Frank Salisbury, the very same picture that Garwell & Kirke had posed for at Scampton back in 1941. Arthur turned to Joan and whispered wryly, *"I should get royalties for that."* His sense of humour was intact, but it masked a deeper problem; he was about to abandon his marriage and his young family. He was going to escape.

The divorce, on the grounds of adultery, became final in November 1956. They'd been married for eleven years. Decree nisi, then decree absolute; I can remember the terms and can remember my mother's deep hurt and bitterness. It was the same year that Frank Sinatra had a hit with a song called 'Love and Marriage.' She hated it, especially the twee rhyme 'love and marriage go together like a horse and carriage.' Her horse had bolted, and she was left alone with two small children.

The 'other woman' was his workplace secretary, Doris. With her fashionably cropped blond hair, high, almost oriental cheekbones, Audrey Hepburn cigarette holder, and ice-cool demeanour, she was as opposite to my mother as it was possible to be; a femme fatale by comparison. He was no longer Arthur to her; she preferred his middle name, John.

It would be easy to cast the wartime hero as the villain of the piece, but even as a young child, I never felt that way. My mother put some of the blame on the war, believing that his harrowing experiences made it hard for him to settle for an ordinary life. That might have been so, but he was also emotionally ill-equipped to meet the challenges of his wife's illness. The dual temptations of his new love and the prospect of a more exciting life overwhelmed him. He moved into her London flat. The bungalow in Bower Hill was left for good.

Epping station again. *"Remember, you must only get off at Liverpool Street. Your dad will be waiting on the platform to meet you."* I can see her waving and blowing a kiss as the doors slide shut and the tube train slowly moves away. I'm eight years old and on my own. I watch through the windows as the green fields of the countryside give way to the prefabs and factories of Debden and the back gardens of London's sprawling suburbs. Station after station passes until the train rattles down into the blackness of the underground tunnel, and there is nothing more to see. I count down the stops until the echoing squeal of the brakes brings the train to a halt at Liverpool Street. Will he be waiting for me? The doors part, and I step onto the platform, straining my eyes anxiously from left to right until I spot him, arms open, calling my name. He sweeps me up into his embrace. *"Hello, Son,"* he says, smiling broadly. He takes me up the escalator and out into the city's quiet weekend streets. We find his car, and he sets off. He's taking me to see something I will never forget.

It only seems to be a few minutes before he stops the car, and we get out. In front of us is a huge rubble-filled crater where buildings once stood. Around it are the shattered, half-collapsed remains of what must have been offices, shops, and houses. The ruins seem to stretch as far as my young eyes can see.

In my mind now, 65 years on, I imagine it as a scene from a film: a long-distance shot takes in the desolate panorama and the two small figures standing beside a black car looking on. It's filmed from behind them. The camera moves closer. A little boy holds tightly onto the slender fingers of his father as wisps of grey smoke drift slowly over the ruins. Nothing is said. Maybe the film will tell the story of the blitz, or maybe the story of the RAF's fight for a nation's survival. Or maybe it will be about the futility of war and the millions of unborn children robbed of a life that the little boy, through the twists of fortune, is living.

We get back in the car, and the mood changes and lifts. We're heading for his manor, the East End. He grins as he breaks into the chorus of an old cockney music hall song; 'boiled beef and carrots, boiled beef and carrots.' We're only sixteen miles from Epping, but it feels like another world. Buildings crowd in on each other along grey, grimy streets. The black bonnet of the Wolseley turns one way then another, until he pulls up outside the peeling facade of a barber's shop. There's a side door that opens to reveal a narrow, gloomy staircase. Taking my hand again, he steps inside, and we go up. He knocks on the door of a flat above the shop, and a gruff voice shouts for us to come in. There, in a large, sparsely furnished room, a scruffily dressed, oldish man beckons us towards a kitchen table and invites us, in a thick cockney accent, to sit down. He puts the kettle on. My father and this man seem to know each other, but I can't quite make out what they are talking about. It just leaves a strange and puzzling impression on my young mind that never goes away.

All these years later, I can still only guess at what connected an ex-RAF Customs and Excise Investigation Officer to the odd, almost Dickensian, character that we met that day. Maybe he was a source in the quest for information on smuggled goods. Who knows? We must have gone to where my dad was living as well, and I must have met Doris for the first time, but of those things, I have not the slightest recollection.

Later that same year, there was another, much longer, train journey. My father had rented a house overlooking the sea at Port Gaverne, on Cornwall's rugged north coast. It was just after Christmas, and this time, my brother, still just four years old, was with me. We waved goodbye to our mother at Paddington station with carefully imparted instructions to get off at Bodmin. It must have been a very sad and lonely journey for her back to an empty house in Bower Hill with no husband and no children. For us kids, though, it was a big adventure, although I only have three clear memories of that holiday with my father and his new partner. The first was the car journey from the station to the clifftop house in Port Gaverne through the bare, bleak, winter landscape of Cornish hills and vales. Then there was my daily walk over the hill to the little bakery in Port Isaac to collect freshly baked bread, still warm, for breakfast. Finally, I remember the wonder of swimming in the sea at Padstow in January. That's all, and then it was back home to mum and the little bungalow in Epping.

Watching out for my little brother and comforting my distressed mother; while I was beginning to take on the role of my absent father, he was about to embark on an adventure he'd dreamed of in Stalag Luft 3. He was going to Africa. For good.

CHAPTER 32

Separate Ways

Stories of bravery and survival in wartime live on, celebrated in books and films, retold time and again. Heroes are fêted with medals and remembered with memorials. But there are other battles, private, hidden, forgotten, unremarkable.

Left alone and with a history of anxiety, depression, and brain surgery, my mother faced a daunting challenge; how would she cope with two small boys, putting food on the table, and paying the bills? The messy business of divorce was over, but there were other issues; emotional as well as financial. She was told that, as a divorced woman, she would no longer be welcome at the local Mother's Union group - a church-based organisation supposedly aimed at promoting the well-being of families. It didn't seem to matter that she was the innocent party; in conservative 1950s Britain, divorce carried a stigma that fostered much tut-tutting behind neighbourhood net curtains. It got her down, but she knew she had one aim in life above all others; to do the best she could for her boys.

There were, of course, the practical things; maintaining the house, taming the huge garden, finding a way to make ends meet. I knew that I could help with the garden: Dad had left an old motor mower that he'd inherited from the cricket club. It was a beast of a machine driven by a temperamental four-stroke petrol engine.

Two sharp triangular blades bolted onto a large rotating disc did the cutting, including, on one memorable occasion, my father's foot. Stopping the motor involved pushing a metal plate onto the exposed spark plug to short-circuit the electrics. Finding out the hard way that on no account should I use a bare hand rather than a booted foot for this operation was a valuable life lesson for one so young. And there were many other minor mishaps of a vaguely comical nature: the day my mother drove a garden fork into a wasp's nest in a quest for a meagre crop of potatoes from the vegetable plot. She was stung as she ran to the bottom of the garden, then, for good measure, stung again on the way back. Not at all funny for her. Then there was the afternoon all three of us spent trapped in the walk-in pantry because the door, which my brother had pulled shut behind us, could only be opened from the outside. Plaintive cries for help through the tiny window finally brought a curious neighbour to the rescue after what seemed like hours.

Our mother wanted desperately to cope, to hide her inner turmoil from us children, but the mental battles she fought could never be successfully concealed – we lived through them with her.

It was early in 1957 when our father packed up his few belongings and moved to Kenya, taking Doris and his ever-faithful golden retriever, Rustler, with him. The job offer was too good to ignore – to set up an investigation and valuation branch for the British East African Customs and Excise Department. It perfectly married the post-war skills he'd acquired working in London with his Stalag Luft 3 dreams of a new life in Africa, but it was a deeply troubled time in the British colony. The Mau Mau uprising started in 1952 when Kikuyu tribesmen, angry at being robbed of their lands by white settlers, embarked on a vicious terror campaign against what they saw as their colonial oppressors. Hidden in the impenetrable bamboo forests on the slopes of Mount Kenya, they launched murderous attacks on isolated farmsteads before disappearing without a trace. The response from the British government was uncompromising; 10,000 regular troops were brought in to try and quell the rebellion, backed up by some 25,000 men of the Kikuyu home guard – tribesmen who'd remained loyal to their colonial rulers. Thousands of suspected Mau Mau sympathisers were herded into detention camps where the interrogation methods employed by the British included beatings, torture, and, it emerged years later, rape. It was a shameful episode in the nation's colonial history. The uprising had been crushed by the time Arthur arrived to take up his post with Customs and Excise, and he would have known nothing about what had gone on in the detention camps. As a survivor of a much more benign prison camp regime, it would have horrified him.

He and Doris set up home in a bungalow on the outskirts of the port city of Mombasa, not far from the clear blue seas of the Indian Ocean. Mombasa was vibrant, multicultural, and, compared to the staid normality of Epping, wildly exotic. In his prison camp letters, he'd jokingly referred to Africa as the 'Dark Continent' but, bathed in brilliant, penetrating sunlight, Mombasa was anything but that. Leaving his two young sons five thousand miles behind was a high price to pay for a new life, but he didn't have to give up all hope of seeing us. There were benefits to being a British civil servant working abroad, and one of them was the Government's willingness to cover the cost of flying the children of its employees to and from the U.K. for their education. He wasted no time in asking our mother if she would agree to let us go for the next six-week summer holiday. It led to some tense exchanges, as this solicitor's letter, which I found in her old, crumpled carrier bag, demonstrates:

'Dear Mrs Garwell,

I have still heard nothing either from Mr Garwell or his solicitors about the outstanding costs of the Maintenance proceedings and of the matter of your children's visit to him this summer. Will you please impress upon him, should you write to him, that he will find that the children are not going out unless he deals properly with the matters outstanding.'

Arthur had to reassure her:

'If you send them, you will have to rely on me to send them back. As I have never made any attempt to contest custody and always have said that they should be with you anyway, what's all the trouble?'

His tone had softened by the end of the letter:

'I am glad the boys liked their little toys. Tim will be at school, no doubt, when you get this. How time flies, doesn't it? Thank Tim for his drawings. We thought they were first class. All the best. Arthur.'

Torn between her fear of, just maybe, losing her boys forever, and her desire for us not to be permanently kept apart from our father, she decided to let us go. Trust in the man she had once loved still flickered somewhere deep inside.

Photo that appeared in the West Essex Gazette newspaper with us in our B.O.A.C. Junior Jet Club T-shirts.

⌒

Arriving at Victoria underground station in July 1957, my mother, flustered and anxious, took my little brother by the hand and, carrying our luggage in the other, made for the crowded escalator. I could feel the rush of hot, sticky air as we headed up towards the bustling London streets above. Stepping into the glare of summer sunshine, she shielded her eyes, looked up and down the crowded pavements for a moment, hesitated, then started walking. People pushed past, horns blared, and everyone seemed to be rushing somewhere, oblivious to the young woman and the two small boys holding onto her tightly. The minutes passed, but soon she could see the building she was looking for; the B.O.A.C. Air Terminal. There it was, in the middle of London, miles from any airport. She stepped into the echoing hush of its elegant, art deco reception hall, knowing that she would soon be waving her sons' goodbye. Only now, writing this, can I begin to imagine how she must have felt as she passed us into the care of the airline's staff.

We were not the only unaccompanied children there that day, but we were not, like many others, seasoned travellers returning from boarding school to spend another summer holiday with ex-pat parents; we were novices, aged nine and five. The British Overseas Airways Corporation, in a desire to cater to this niche market, had launched what they called 'The Junior Jet Club,' and we were now proud members. Decked out in our bright yellow Junior Jet Club T-shirts and with our club badges and logbooks, we were ready for the big adventure. As our coach pulled out into the morning traffic, bound for London airport, we watched as our mother, waving, disappeared from view.

It might have been called the Junior Jet Club, but there would be no jetting for us; we were flying to Nairobi in a propeller plane, the Douglas DC-4 or Argonaut. We didn't know it then, but the military version of the aircraft had been used in the Berlin Airlift soon after World War II. It was, like the Lancaster, powered by four Rolls Royce Merlin engines. Settling into our seats and hoping that we wouldn't need the sick bags stowed in the pocket in front of us, we watched through the windows as each of the engines spluttered in turn, then, with a puff of blue smoke, roared into life. Slowly the aircraft edged its way to the end of the runway, turned, and stopped. We waited. The low growl of the engines gradually grew and grew until the noise reached a howling crescendo, and the aircraft strained every sinew to be free. It would have been a sensation our father experienced time after time, but that never crossed our minds. Then it was as if the pilot had let the handbrake off; the plane leapt forward, the airport buildings seemed to flash past our window with ever-increasing speed, and suddenly we were airborne and looking down at the houses and streets below and then the patchwork fields and towns of southern England. Next stop, Rome.

Climbing up into clouds, the plane briefly bumped and shook like a fairground ride but then broke free of the turbulence and headed into the clear blue sky above, the four engines settling into a monotonous drone. Hours passed. The sick bags stayed where they were. It was lunchtime when we came into land in Rome and were led into the transit lounge while the aircraft was refuelled. An hour later, after ice cream, we were looking down at the Mediterranean Sea as the Argonaut headed for Benghazi on the coast of North Africa. It took another five hours to get there, plenty of time for the children on board to take it in turns to visit the flight deck and for the pilot to joke that my five-year-old brother, invited to briefly take the controls, had steered the aircraft off course. We eventually landed at Benghazi, and Tim, much to his surprise, still hadn't been sick.

After more refuelling and more waiting in the airport lounge, it was up and away again as the setting sun slipped toward the horizon and the Nile River glinted below us. We headed into the darkness and tried to sleep. It was the middle of the night when the Argonaut came into land at Khartoum in Sudan, and we stepped, bleary-eyed, into a wall of hot Saharan air filled with the sound of chirping crickets and the pungent smell of aviation fuel. Taking my brother by the hand, a stewardess led us across the tarmac into the airport lounge and sat us down at a table. Giant fans revolved slowly above our heads as a waiter, dressed in a long white tunic and a bright red fez, brought us soft drinks. It was all very exotic for two young children from Essex who'd never been abroad before.

I can't remember much more of the journey. The Argonaut flew on through the long night as my brother and I slept fitfully. Then dawn broke, and we peered down at an empty African landscape. Two stops to go: Entebbe in Uganda, then, finally, Nairobi, the capital city of Kenya. Except that it wasn't the final stop: twenty-three hours after leaving Heathrow, we still had one more flight to go, this time in an old twin-engined Dakota for the last three-hundred-mile leg of the journey to meet dad. As we stepped out of the Dakota into the blinding light of Mombasa, my brother, with not a sick bag in sight, finally threw up.

I can remember waking up the next morning after our first night's sleep and seeing a monkey sitting in a mango tree in the garden of dad's rented bungalow. Welcome to Kenya. Six weeks later, we were back in England. It was as if it had all been a dream.

Dad, Doris & Rustler - Mombasa 1957.

Me, Tim, and a new friend - Mombasa 1957.

The bungalow with Mango trees in the garden.

Photo sent to John & Tim from Daddy with love. 20-3-57.

CHAPTER 33

Making Ends Meet

Forty pounds a month was not going to be enough to keep a house and feed two growing lads, even back then, but that was all our mum received in alimony. The bungalow had been offered to her for purchase at a price of £1,200, so there was a mortgage to pay as well. She tried to hide her anxiety but could never quite manage it, so I gradually began to take on the role of the man of the house. Where could some extra money come from? The bungalow only had two bedrooms, but there was a sitting room with a bay window and a fireplace – maybe that could be rented out to a lodger. And so, it came to be. Old Mrs Sargeant was the first, and to us boys, she seemed truly ancient – and grumpy. Not that we helped, tearing noisily around the front garden on our bikes, right under her window. It never occurred to us to think what a sad and lonely way it was for her to end up. After she left to go who knows where, the room was rented by an elderly man called Bill Bozier, who earned a meagre living doing gardening jobs around Epping. He was a large, gentle fellow with a ruddy complexion and two odd habits: the first had mum and us trying to keep a straight face when, every morning around the breakfast table, he ceremoniously poured his tea onto his bowl of cornflakes, rather than into his cup. The other was less amusing: coming home in the afternoon from a hard day's gardening, he liked to hang his ancient, sweat-stained, flat cap on the back doorknob inside the kitchen, where it emitted a smell that was beyond description. None of us dared touch it. For ages, mum was too polite to complain, not wanting to hurt the poor man's feelings, but eventually, she succumbed, much to our relief. Eventually, he left too.

Then, on one sunny summer's day came a knock on the front door that would change her life. Two women stood there; one was short, plump, bespectacled, and jovial; the other, tall and thin with strikingly aquiline features. Betty Williams and Jane Stevens were holding magazines – 'The Watchtower' and 'Awake!' - and had come to preach the good news, but they met a frosty, almost angry reception. Chucked out of the Mothers Union, disillusioned with the church, and hurt by her failed marriage, our once believing mother had little time for religion. That might have been the end of it, but Betty, who'd not long returned from missionary work in fiercely Catholic Ireland, and Oxford-educated Jane, who'd had an even tougher challenge preaching to the native population of New Guinea where cannibalism, it is said, had not been fully eradicated, were not easily put off. With their gentle coaxing, she opened her heart and poured out her feelings. The turning point came when they showed her that, according to the bible, her husband's adultery was, unlike what she'd been told, legitimate grounds for divorce. They asked if they could come back and talk to her again. They did, and that's how, in time, she became a Jehovah's Witness. There were bible studies, sometimes in our back garden on warm days, and meetings in a dingy back room of the Mechanics Institute in Hemnall Street with my brother and I tagging along. It gave her a belief, a reason for hope, and a tightly knit support network of fellow believers - things that would go on to sustain her for the rest of her life. Betty and Jane, meanwhile, carried on with their mission to convert the local population, pedalling around the Essex lanes on their bicycles with the Watchtower and Awake magazines stuffed into the bags on their handlebars. Once a fledgling congregation had been established, they were sent, so it was said, where the need was greater.

Support for our sometimes-struggling mother came from other directions, too, though not very often. Her father, Albert, who had long since been crippled with multiple sclerosis, came to visit from his home in Oldham. It seemed incredible then, and it still does now, to think that he made the round trip of four hundred miles in his pale blue, single-seater, three-wheeled, invalid car with its tiny 147cc engine, barely powerful enough to propel a small motorcycle, but that's what he did. Her blond-haired, war-wounded brother, Peter, visited too. Now married with a daughter and living in Doncaster, his presence always lifted the mood at 51 Bower Hill. From teaching us kids how to ride our bikes by letting go of the saddle without telling us to demonstrating how to blow up a large screw-top metal drum with a penny banger, he was, when he was there, just like a surrogate father. There was a lot of laughter.

Money was still very tight. Every purchase, from a new vacuum cleaner to a twin-tub washing machine, had to be carefully considered and paid for in instalments. When the pebbledash bungalow desperately needed repainting, there was no chance of paying for a decorator, so she bought a large tin of Snowcem masonry paint and tackled the job herself. I can picture her now balancing on a small wooden ladder with paint-splattered spectacles and hair wrapped in a headscarf. The windows were cleaned for free in return for letting George, the local window cleaner, and his mate store their ladders in the back garden. Whether George harboured a faint hope of other favours from this young, still attractive divorcee when he popped in for a mid-round cup of tea, it's impossible to say, but I'd like to think that his motives were pure.

We had a few 'odd' visitors, though; one, in the early days, looking furtive, knocked on the front door and asked if Arthur had left anything for him to collect. He walked disconsolately away when he learned that Arthur didn't live there anymore. What a London-based Customs and Excise Investigation Officer might have that would elicit the visitor's interest could only be surmised, but it was most likely of a pictorial nature and illicit.

There were no male friends hovering around, no ardent admirers. Deep disillusionment over the abandonment by her first love saw to that. She'd had enough of men in that way, for the time being. Her focus was on looking after her boys and making ends meet financially. Instead of buying tinned food for the cat, she chose to boil up what were called lights – better known as lungs – bought cheaply and raw from the local butcher. Bubbling and foaming in a large pan on top of the cooker, they looked and smelled evil. Chopped into leathery cubes after cooking, the cat seemed to like them well enough, but then, the cat enjoyed dismembering rats and leaving them, half-eaten, under our beds as well.

Beneath the draining board in the kitchen, behind a yellow gingham curtain, lurked a repository for a collection of old, yellow, Marigold rubber gloves, most of them punctured, some with a finger end missing. She couldn't bring herself to throw them away - just in case. Looking for anything else under there usually involved a fight with a pile of rubber gloves as they made a vain bid for freedom.

The bungalow was hard to keep warm, especially in the freezing winter of 1963, the coldest in over two hundred years. Frost formed on the inside of the bedroom windows as hedge-high, ice-topped snow drifts covered the countryside for weeks on end. The solid fuel stove in the living room struggled to make much impression, and a small paraffin heater brought in for reinforcement gave off little more than a fumey smell. I can't remember giving much thought to my father back then or thinking how different his life in the heat of Kenya must have been to ours in Epping; he'd become emotionally as well as literally distant. If I did, I felt no resentment, no sense of being abandoned. It was just how it was.

'23rd December 1960

Dear John & Tim,

We were very pleased to have your last letters and the very good pictures of yourselves that you sent. The snaps I am sending are being forwarded by my father so that you can see some of our animals. We also have two pigs now!

I hope you both have a very happy Christmas and also that you have received the parcel we sent. Daddy sends his love to you and will write soon.

Love from Aunty Doris.'

It seemed that Doris was still acting as his secretary.

For a while, Dad paid for my brother Tim to go to a private

school. It was four tube train stops away in upmarket Buckhurst Hill. Mum took him on the first day but, typically independent, although only seven years old, he insisted on making his own way there the following day. It was quite a long walk from the station to Daiglen school, and, not having paid enough attention the previous day, he got hopelessly lost, gave up the quest, and, in his smart new uniform, made his way back home. The brief spell of private education only lasted until the money to pay for it dried up. Then it was off to the local junior school, where the other pupils singled him out as a posh boy and picked on him.

The back garden, all half an acre of it, gradually went wild. The chickens and their wooden coop had long gone, and the vegetable patch disappeared under a blanket of long grass and nettles. All that remained of its old self was a patch of infrequently mowed lawn at the back and the square flower bed at the front with its scraggly, weed-threatened rose bushes. It made a great adventure playground for us kids. Much amusement could be had with a box of matches and a wilderness of tinder-dry grass until we accidentally set fire to our next-door neighbour's hedge. We built barricades and fought battles, rolling old car tyres at each other's encampments. I've no idea where the tyres came from, but I do recall an old, dilapidated, home-built sports car being dumped in the back garden by a friend of a friend of Dad's - it was red, rusty, and useless, but great fun as a plaything.

For a while, Mum worked part-time in a decorating shop on Epping's high street, but then the shop closed. Next, she found an office job at Stapleford Tawney Aerodrome, but that was five miles away down country lanes, and she couldn't drive. An old 49cc pedal-assisted Mobylette moped rescued the situation, and she'd wobble away from Bower Hill trailing blue smoke with her crash helmet at a jaunty angle and L-plates flapping in the breeze. That job stopped soon enough too.

It was tough for her, and she struggled to cope. There were periods of depression and tearful episodes of wondering how she'd get through it all. But I remember laughter too, and how she loved to sing when the blackness lifted. She wouldn't give up on her boys, not for anything.

CHAPTER 34

Kenyan Adventures

In 1958, Dad and Doris moved from Mombasa to Kenya's capital, Nairobi. He'd been asked to form a customs investigation and valuation branch for the whole of British East Africa - Kenya, Tanganyika, and Uganda - so he set about recruiting a team of trustworthy officers to take on the task. Maybe there were distant echoes of gathering together a crew to fly Hampden bombers for 83 Squadron back in 1940 - although with a much better chance of survival. Like so many other ex-prisoners of Stalag Luft 3, Ginger Garwell was a high achiever - and a natural leader. His wartime fear that he might end up *as a rather deadbeat, red-nosed, Customs officer wearing a battered bowler and pin-striped pants'* proved to be ill-founded. He was up for an adventure.

The road from Nairobi to Kiambu heads due north. Leaving the city's bustling centre where the colonial government buildings, Asian-owned shops, and pavement-squatting beggars seem to fight for space, we head through the sprawling, run-down suburbs and out into rural Africa. The ribbon of road, edged on each side by red, dusty soil, cuts through the Karura Forest, its tall trees briefly shading us from the heat of the sun. Past scattered roadside shacks, wandering rib-thin cattle, and walkers bent under heavy loads, dad's pale blue American V8 Ford soon passes through Kiambu town to the hill country beyond where the coffee grows. Turning left off the main road, we sweep up a dirt track, billowing dust clouds behind us. Ahead, perched on top of a hill, is a single-storey house with an arched veranda shining white in the midday sun. The dogs, Rhodesian Ridgebacks, bound out to greet us, barking noisily. There are flower beds of vivid red and pink bougainvillea, lawns dotted with fruit trees, and a shimmering blue swimming pool. We tumble eagerly out of the car and look around in renewed amazement; our dad lives here!

It was 1963 and our third trip to Kenya; I was fifteen years old, my brother eleven. The list of aircraft in our Junior Jet Club logbooks tracked the rapid progress of international aviation: from the old propellor-driven Argonaut to the much faster Bristol Britannia Turboprop and then the de Havilland Comet, the world's first commercial jet airliner. We were getting to be old hands at air travel. The white villa and the coffee plantation surrounding it sat at 6,000 feet above sea level. On a clear day, the snow-topped twin peaks of Mount Kenya could be seen on the horizon, quivering in the heat haze one hundred miles to the north. Not content to settle for a lifetime as a civil servant, and with the prospect of Kenyan independence looming, his decision to buy the small plantation and grow coffee as a side-line made sense. But it wasn't just coffee; to the back of the house, beyond the double garages and the kitchen courtyard, were two huge, windowless sheds. In their dark, humid interiors stood long rows of stacked shelves loaded with deep trays of black compost – and mushrooms. He'd set up the business himself, importing the first spawn from the U.K. with the intention of supplying the hotel trade across Kenya and beyond. He called the business Amberley Mushrooms. There was no lack of ambition. The growing of mushrooms required copious quantities of horse manure, which, when sourced, was collected in the car. Once the cavernous boot was filled, it was shovelled onto the back seat until it reached the roof. He'd smile when he told us how he'd poke a hole through with a long stick so he could still use the rear-view mirror. We believed him. Of course we did.

My father and I were not close; how could we be? He lived for the moment, never speaking of his earlier days in Epping or of my mother, and certainly not of his wartime experiences. He preferred to joke with his two boys, like laughing over our refusal to eat an avocado pear, a fruit we'd never seen before. *"One of those would cost you two shillings and sixpence at Fortnum and Mason,"* he would tease, increasing the amount each time he said it. His occasional bravura performance of underarm fart noises amused us immensely – as did the post-meal belching competitions he liked to initiate. A hark back to room seven shenanigans at Stalag Luft 3, perhaps?

The dinner table at Kiambu was often spread with what seemed to us strangely exotic fare. It was prepared by David, the Kikuyu cook. I can remember large bowls of freshly chopped pineapple submerged in double cream, rich food unlike anything we'd tasted at Bower Hill. No wonder Dad had put on weight; he was no longer the thin 'greyhound breed' figure he once was. The house was nothing like Bower Hill's modest 1930s bungalow: fitted mahogany bookshelves along one wall of the spacious sitting room stretched from the polished parquet floor to the ceiling; glazed doors on two sides opened onto the quarry tiled wrap-around veranda with its striking white arches, like some Spanish villa on the Costa Blanca. As I reach deeper into the dusty filing cabinet of memories, I can picture Dad sitting there in his armchair enjoying a glass or two of whisky. There were two large kitchens and numerous bedrooms that opened from a long corridor. Despite the appearance of wealth, Dad was unpretentious, down-to-earth, and well-liked by his African workers on the plantation. I liked him too; we both did.

Like most kids back then, Tim and I didn't choose to spend much time indoors, not when we had such a huge playground to explore. We'd run through the coffee bushes with their ripening red berries, sometimes stopping to watch the Kikuyu women as they tended to the crop, their voices joined together in rhythmic song. The plantation workers lived with their families in a row of traditional mud-walled, grass-roofed huts on the estate. We'd visit them often, and they'd beckon us inside to sit by an open fire in the gloomy interior as they prepared food and chatted away in Swahili.

There were adventures away from Kiambu as well. One of Dad's friends, a work colleague, had a house at Nanyuki, 120 miles to the north. It was close to the equator and in the shadow of the giant, jagged peaks of Mount Kenya. We went for a short stay, just the two of us with Dad's friend, stopping for a photograph as we crossed the equator. The house in Nanyuki had steel bars protecting the windows - a reminder of the fear felt by white settlers when Mau-Mau terrorists launched random attacks from their hiding places deep in the impenetrable bamboo forests on the slopes of the mountain. The uprising was over, but the steel bars remained. We were taken up the mountain until the car reached the bamboo zone at 10,000 feet and ran out of road. It was deserted, and the dark, dense, towering bamboo felt strangely threatening. We could go no further, so the car was turned around to descend the 4,000 feet back to Nanyuki, where the after-effects of the altitude brought tiredness, then sleep.

At the equator on the road trip to Nanyuki.

Once back at Kiambu, there was yet more to see. The lions, giraffes, and gazelles of the Nairobi National Park were memorable, but one trip remains as fresh in the mind as if it happened yesterday, not some sixty years ago.

We scrambled into the back seat of the big blue Ford, ready for the journey ahead. I sat by one window and Tim by the other. Between us, dressed in his best white shirt, sat David, the cook. Dad stowed our suitcases in the boot, slipped into the driver's seat next to Doris, lit a cigarette, and set off. We passed through Kiambu town, then the bustling centre of Nairobi, and out onto the main road to Mombasa, 300 miles away. The powerful V8 engine seemed to eat up the miles effortlessly, and cruising along the smooth tarmac at 80 mph, we felt like kings of the road. Then it all changed. After sixty miles, the tarmac came to an end, and the dirt road started. The speed dropped, and the wheels started throwing up clouds of red dust. The road ahead seemed to rise and fall endlessly as it cut through the vast, empty plains dotted with Acacia trees.

The first smell of burning rubber was slight but soon became overwhelming. Wisps of blue smoke appeared from nowhere. Dad pulled the car into the side of the road, stopped, got out, and lifted the bonnet. Nothing amiss there. Puzzled, he ushered us out and proceeded to remove a series of rubber mats of varying age and thickness from the rear seat well to reveal a hole in the floor. It was big enough to see the road below us and a very large, very hot exhaust pipe. So that was the problem. The mats were discarded, but the hole remained – and the journey continued with 200 miles still to go.

The windows were all down. Dad, with one arm resting on the open windowsill and the other holding the steering wheel, looked calm, unflustered. Doris, her eyes concealed behind film star sunglasses, seemed inscrutable. I was leaning out of one back window, Tim the other, but David, the cook, was stuck in the middle. As clouds of dust billowed into the car, his best white shirt and closely cropped black hair slowly turned a deep shade of terracotta red. He didn't seem to mind.

Arriving hot and sticky in Mombasa, dad headed straight for the cool, spacious bar of the Mombasa Sports Club, a grand art deco building with colonial overtones surrounded by lush green, tree-lined playing fields. With drinks ordered from a waiter in a spotless white jacket, he and Doris settled down to wait for their friends and wash away the lingering dust with a stiff drink or two, while Tim and I quickly downed our Coca-Colas and headed out to explore the grounds.

Another family – husband, wife, and son – were travelling separately from Nairobi and joining us for our holiday. As white settlers in Kenya, they knew the country well, and their son, a little older than me, had a slightly arrogant air of self-confidence about him. The bungalow we were all to stay in was away from the city and close to the silver beaches of the Indian Ocean. It sat in a clearing surrounded by trees with no other houses close by. There were only enough beds in the place for four adults and two children, so a flysheet and a camp bed with a mosquito net were set up on the flat roof, which was accessed from outside the house by means of a concrete staircase. We kids were to take turns to sleep up there under the stars with nothing but the mysterious sounds and occasional screeches of the African night to punctuate the silence and, just when it happened to be my turn, a violent thunderstorm. My frantic banging on the door in the middle of the night was thankfully heard above the torrential rain.

The beach, a quarter of a mile away, could be reached on foot by taking a narrow, grassy pathway through thick undergrowth and overhanging trees. We were told to watch out for snakes but arriving at the ocean's edge and slipping into the warm, turquoise waters with a snorkel and goggles to see the dazzlingly-coloured marine life in the deep rock pools on the coral reef made any risk of treading on something venomous seem insignificant.

The beach was fine, but the bar of the Mombasa Sports Club held an almost equal attraction for the adults of the party. They seemed to spend hours there while we kicked around the perimeter of the cricket pitches and playing fields, getting bored. It felt a bit like when we were perched on the back seat of the Wolseley with crisps and tomato juice outside the Spotted Dog pub in Epping years before. Finally, we were told, *"Go and explore the market if you don't know what to do."* So, we did - and then the adventure really began.

It was about half a mile away down narrow streets crowded with locals. Left here, right there, three of us together, but only one of us with any idea of where to go. Suddenly, at the far end of the street, we heard a loud commotion, then saw a figure in a long white robe running away from an angry crowd of Africans. *"Quick, down here!"* our new friend shouted as he pointed at a narrow alleyway off to our right. He ran, and we followed, away, or so I thought, from trouble. More tight turns, more changes of direction until we were suddenly confronted by the fugitive sprinting head-on towards the three of us with the mob hot on his heels. It was too late to turn around, and with nowhere else to go, we stopped dead. As the fleeing man drew level with us, my ginger-haired little brother stuck his foot out to trip him up. It was easily avoided, but a few yards further on, the man was surrounded and stopped. The African market stall holders, angrily accusing the Arab of theft, crowded around him with apparently violent intent. It was at this precise moment that Tim decided to elbow his way to the front of the crush to get a better view. I grabbed his shoulder to hold him back just as the Arab pulled out a curved dagger and raised it above his head. The crowd shrank back with a collective gasp – and then the police arrived. The drama was over.

We still went to the market, at least I think we did. When we finally returned to the Mombasa Sports Club, the grownups were sitting at the bar exactly where we'd left them, drinks in hand, blissfully ignorant. If there's one thing our brush with danger proved, it was that, of the two of us, my brother was most like my father – and it wasn't just the ginger hair.

In December 1963, Kenya gained its independence and Jomo Kenyatta, previously imprisoned as a Mau-Mau activist, became the country's first Prime Minister, then President. Colonial rule was over.

No longer the greyhound look. Dad, whisky in hand,
& Doris watching a cricket match in 1964.

CHAPTER 35

Highs and Lows -
the Final Letters

It was cold and raining when my brother and I arrived back in London. Heavy grey clouds hung low over the airport, pushing the dazzling light and heat of Africa away as if it had all been a dream. Our mother was there to meet us, arms eagerly outstretched, but I felt overwhelmed by the contrast, the drabness, and couldn't quite hide it. I hoped she wouldn't notice, but she did, of course. What I couldn't have known then is that we would never see our father again.

It was over a year later, in April 1965, when an airmail letter in dad's distinctive handwriting dropped through our letter box at Bower Hill, addressed to my brother and me.

'Dear John & Tim,

Thank you for your letter. I was pleased to hear that everything is going alright with you all. I trust that you, John, are polishing your windows properly. With any luck, we might have another George Formby in the family.'

This requires some explanation. I'd just left school and, although long since gone, had a young person's zeal for the religion that seemed to have rescued my mother. With a firmly held belief that what the bible called Armageddon was just around the corner,

I, like all other young JW's, was encouraged to go and knock on doors in a quest for converts rather than pursue further education and a career. Window cleaning was the part-time job of choice for many of us. His sarcastic humour stung a bit, but didn't dent the certainty I had back then that I was doing the right thing. Then he wrote something that could have cut much deeper:

> 'Doris and I have adopted - not legally but in fact - a small boy of about eight or nine whose mother was Kikuyu and father European. The father was killed in an air crash. His name is David, and he is a very bright little boy.'

Two boys abandoned, one boy rescued. Reading the letter now, I might see it that way but have no memory of being hurt by it then. I felt no resentment, not consciously anyway. The subject was quickly changed:

> 'I am still working with Customs, having just signed another contract for two years. As we are Kenyan citizens, it is probable that they will want me to carry on for some years yet.
>
> The coffee is now excellent, and we will pick our first real crop this year - possibly three tons or more. Mushrooms have been good, and we have picked over 3,000 lbs since Christmas. They are dropping off a bit now as we have the long rains, and it is a bit colder than usual. Fortunately, it nearly always rains during the night and is hot with plenty of sunshine during the day.
>
> We had three days down at Mombasa recently. It was very pleasant.
>
> By the way, we have sold the Mercedes and the Ford and now have a Citroen ID19, which is a very nice car indeed - although the gearbox went just the other day, and it is going to cost £70 to repair.
>
> With love and best wishes. Dad and Aunty Doris.'

By the end of the year, the mood had changed completely; the alimony payments had ground to a halt, and Mum had written to query it. The reply she received betrayed both frustration and anger:

'Dear Joan,

I am sorry about the fact that you didn't get paid this month. The position is that I did not have enough funds to meet the banker's order. Although you might think I am very well off, I am, in fact, extremely poor.'

He then provided a detailed list of income and expenditure to try and prove the point, ending with:

'...leaving me about £100 from which I have to pay wages which this month amount to £115. It is, therefore, impossible. My income depends on mushrooms, and they are variable - and coffee, but the crop is picked annually. I cannot, therefore, see why John should not get a reasonable job instead of frigging about two days a week only. I quite understand that you cannot do a full-time job and run the house as well. Anyway, I know one or two Witnesses here - one is on my staff - and they all do a full day's work and the rest of the business in the evenings and weekends. I agreed to pay for John and Tim to carry on at school, thinking that they would thereby improve themselves and obtain good jobs, not become window cleaners. I cannot see how it is possible for me to pay more than £20 a month - I can't even see how I can manage that, but I will try. In about a year's time, I will have bought my house. Then things should be a little easier.'

He ends abruptly there with no signature.

That letter hurt then, and it still hurts now, all these years later. Disappointing a father, even an absent one, is tough. The thing is,

I understand how he felt. I wish I could tell him. I wish he knew that I soon gave up *'frigging about'* and got a proper full-time office job in the City of London to support my mum, but he never did.

By the following year – 1966 – things had improved:

'Dear Joan, John & Tim,

I am sorry for the delay in writing to you all. It must be Africa.

Things are going well here - coffee's growing well, mushrooms not too well. They, however, vary from crop to crop. I am still with the Investigation Branch and may get one more two-year contract, starting next February.

I have recently changed my bank to the Ottoman and made a Bankers Order in your favour payable to your account at Barclays, Epping. There should therefore be no break in payments.

I am very pleased, Tim, that you did so well at school. I am sorry that I cannot have you out here on holiday as I am now a Kenyan citizen and I have, therefore, to pay the fare myself. However, we may be able to manage this next year. I am sure that young David - the boy we have adopted - not legally yet - would be delighted to see you. No news of John. How is he doing?

Had a letter from Nora. She is still at 'Viewlands,' and the old folks are apparently going strong. Reckon they will have to shoot them eventually.

Love. John & Doris.'

His sense of humour seemed to be fully recovered.

It was now 1967. Back in Britain, the 'Swinging Sixties' was in full flow: the Beatles had released 'Sergeant Pepper' and Jimmy

Hendrix had recorded 'Purple Haze.' Mick Jagger and Keith Richards had been arrested on drugs charges, then acquitted, and London's Carnaby Street remained the epicentre of youth fashion – it was a time of social upheaval and the 'permissive society,' but not in Kenya. John Garwell, ex-RAF bomber pilot, was now a citizen of that country. He'd hoped for a life in Africa when imprisoned in Stalag Luft 3 all those years ago, and that hope had been fulfilled, just not with the woman he'd first fallen in love with. Now he was in love with Kenya:

'29th March 1967

Dear Nora,

I must immediately apologise for being so slow in writing to you. It must be Africa or the attitude of maybe just me. I do hope that you are well and the old folks. One day you must come here and see us. This is probably the most beautiful country on this earth, and we have one of the most lovely houses in Kenya. My job has just been Africanised and will be taken over by an Assistant Commissioner of Police. I am, therefore, a farmer growing coffee and mushrooms. We have twenty acres - seventeen for coffee and about two acres of lawns, grounds, etc. We can grow anything here - grapes, peaches, apples, oranges, lemons, tangerines, pomegranates, paw-paw, avocado pears, limes, plus, of course, all the European vegetables.'

Sagan's prison camp had offered no such abundance – he'd written from there:

'The garden here has been a bit of a failure. The heat combined with the poor soil - which is pure sand - made failure pretty certain anyway. We hope to get about 30 tomatoes plus a few cabbages and maybe a potato or two.'

He continues:

> 'This really is a remarkable country. At this moment, from my chair
> in the lounge, I can see Mt. Kenya, which is on the Equator and is
> 100 miles away. It has snow on its two peaks.
>
> Doris and I are both Kenyans - no longer British. We have adopted a
> small boy whose mother is Kikuyu - the same tribe as Jomo Kenyatta
> - and whose father was European and died some years ago. He is a
> nice kid and is now about ten. He gets on very well with Doris and
> now with me. At first, he was afraid of me but isn't any longer. At
> 47, I am what is called in Swahili a 'Mzee' or old man. I am just
> beginning to get silver threads amongst the gold. We get on extremely
> well with the Africans - me more so than Doris.
>
> A big laugh for you: I have twice appeared on television - once to talk
> about the RAF and once about the Investigation Branch. A harassing
> experience.'

He doesn't mention it here, but he'd also been featured in the
Kenyan press, photographed meeting an ex-Luftwaffe fighter
pilot. By some unlikely coincidence, it turned out that they'd
been in direct combat with each other during the war. Could it
have been on the Augsburg raid? I don't know the answer to that
and, sadly, the newspaper cutting was lost many years ago.

As a final, almost throw away, piece of news, he writes:

> 'We had a 7ft 6 inches spitting cobra on the veranda the other night.
> The dogs killed it, but they had serious eye trouble.
>
> Love to you and Dad & Mum.
>
> John & Doris.'

So, he'd ended up as a farmer, having written from Stalag Luft 3:

'Farming seems the most popular idea of post-war occupation. I must admit that I have often thought of it myself.'

As he feared it would, his Customs job had gone to an indigenous African, so, in a typically mischievous gesture, he made a point of parking his car, full to the roof with horse manure, on the gleaming white steps of Government House in Nairobi with a plume of pungent steam gently drifting up from the open windows. It amused him no end.

It was two years later when he wrote this, his final letter, addressed to his family at 'Viewlands':

'21st February 1969

Dear Mum, Dad & Nora,

I must apologise for not writing to you for so very long, neither at Christmas time nor on Mum's birthday. How old are you now, Mum? I assume 79 and Dad 82 in May. Doris, incidentally, is 43 today.

Times have been somewhat difficult for us recently as my post was 'Africanised' and my mushroom farm burned down completely. We, therefore, had to sell the farm but only got half the price - £5,000 & £5,000 over a long period - £10,000 in all.

However, to look on the brighter side, they want me to start an Investigation and Valuation branch in Ethiopia, or Abyssinia as it used to be, but the date of starting I don't know yet. Doris can also earn a lot of money up there as a secretary. We are hoping that it will come off soon. My salary will be £3,000 a year, and Doris can get up to £200 a month if she works for an American company.

I hope you can read this as I have always been used to a secretary and have forgotten the art.

I trust that you are all well. I reckon the Northumbrians are so tough that they have to shoot them before burial.

Love. John & Doris.'

In less than a week, he was dead. It was said that he'd had a heart attack when chasing after one of his dogs, but I don't know for sure. He was just 49 years old.

The shocking news was received at 'Viewlands' on a cold winter's day. Nora broke it to her father as he was lighting a coal fire in the dining room. She said he sank to his knees and started to cry.

It was early in the morning when we heard at Bower Hill. I was about to set off to my office job in London, and there was no time for the news to sink in before I got on my Honda 50 and left. I felt numb at first, but somewhere on the old A11, as it cut through the leafless trees of Epping Forest between the Wakes Arms and Robin Hood pubs, it hit me. Tears ran briefly down my ice-cold face. I wiped them away with a gloved hand and carried on into the rush hour traffic of another working day.

His obituary appeared in the East African Standard on 7th March 1969. In two columns, it set out the remarkable events of his life: the raids over enemy territory piloting Hampden bombers; the famous Augsburg raid and the fatal crash in his burning Lancaster; his time in Stalag Luft 3; his escape, recapture, and punishment; his medals; his move to Kenya. It concluded:

John Garwell made many friends and was always ready to extend a helping hand to his fellow men. He won the admiration and regard of all his fellow officers and kept it even after his post was Africanised in 1967. His funeral was attended by several of his officers who had been selected by him and counted themselves his friends. They came together from all three East African countries to pay their final respects. He was carried to his grave by five of his "boys," as he liked to call them, assisted by a close friend.

His funeral was also attended by many of his African friends and employees from his farm, and floral tributes were received from many friends.

Although John Garwell was only in Kenya for twelve years, he leaves a noticeable gap behind him and will be missed for a long time to come, both in Nairobi and in his home at Kiambu. He leaves a widow in Nairobi and two sons in the United Kingdom.'

He was buried at St Paul's church in Kiambu. The gravestone bears this inscription:

'In loving memory of Arthur John Garwell DFC, DFM. He walked with kings... ne'er lost the common touch. Acomb 1920 - Kiambu 1969.'

Epilogue

April 2022. Rain falls gently from a slate grey sky. The wet road twists sharply up through the overhanging trees of Oakwood Bank, up past the last few scattered houses, and brings us, at the end of our journey, to 'Viewlands.' It stands there, alone and unoccupied. The rusting white gate opens onto the same flagstone path that Arthur and his bride-to-be trod in 1945. Weeds thrive where flowers once grew. Tim places a key in the back door and turns it carefully. There are cobwebs in the nooks and crannies of the old wooden porch. Gently pushing the door open, we step into a house frozen in time: the old oak sideboard in the dining room; the writing bureau with its shelves of faded books behind leaded glass doors; the seat in the bay window. All unchanged. We go from room to room, each one bringing back childhood memories. *'Home is so sad,'* the poet Philip Larkin wrote, *'It stays as it was left, shaped to the comfort of the last to go as if to win them back.'* That's exactly how it feels.

In a bedroom cabinet, we find a drawer of family memorabilia, untouched for many years. There are old photographs, certificates, letters, a few French coins from the first World War, and two German coins, the Swastikas clear to see. Tucked away towards the bottom of the drawer, we find a letter. The handwriting is neat and easy to read, and the English is almost perfect. Dated 18th August 1948, it is from Stuttgart, Germany. The name of the sender is Fritz Frasch.

'Dear Mr and Mrs Garwell,

Perhaps you remember the POW who was working in your garden in April 1946, two and a half years ago, and whom you were calling "Fred," who was very tall (6ft 3ins) and had, once upon a morning, a thorn in his finger, which was removed by you, Mrs Garwell. Well, it has been a very long time since those days. But I did not forget your kindness and your helpfulness. I returned home at the end of June 1948 after having spent the very last weeks in the environs of London and having visited the enormous city seven times.

Just now I have begun to write to all the people whom I got to know in your country. It's not a small number of people whom I shall be writing to. And there has been no one who was unfriendly or anything like that. And so, I must express my thanks in writing to all of them. I hope very much that this time the mutual understanding has reached a higher stage than ever before - the disaster has been terrible enough for both sides.

I do not want to forget your little daughter, who will be now about fifteen years old, isn't she?'

He'd sent her some stamps, including some from the time of runaway inflation when a stamp cost millions of German marks. He asked if she could send him one from the London Olympic Games, held that same year. Normal life was slowly returning to a war-ravaged World. He ends the letter with:

'I would enjoy it very much if anybody in your family would write to me again. Now I give you my best wishes for health and happiness and many greetings for you and your daughter.

Yours very sincerely.

Fred.'

There is a second letter, addressed to Nora in 1949 to thank her for the stamps she'd sent. It includes this:

'Do you also learn foreign languages? I learned Latin, Greek, French, and English at school'

The letter concludes:

'Well, three years have passed now since I have been working in your garden. I remember with pleasure those days. Your mother especially warned me often of the bees in your garden. I remember with pleasure her and your father's kindness and helpfulness. Please give my kind regards to your parents and many thanks for their kind letter and for the good wishes from you all for Christmas and the New Year.

Yours most sincerely,

Fred.'

Franz Frisch - an educated, kind, thoughtful man pitched into a war that he, like so many others, didn't want - all because of the twisted ideology of a tyrant.

Before we leave, I stand for a while in the bay window and look out over the Tyne valley and the rolling Pennine hills beyond as the soft rain continues to fall. I think of the futility of war and the millions of lives lost. I think of my father. I think of his bravery, his survival against the odds, and I feel pride in a father I barely knew. Then I think of my mother, how she suffered yet survived her own battles, never giving up on her two children, however hard it got. A hero in a different kind of war; unsung, undecorated.

Acknowledgements

I am indebted to everyone who helped me in some way, great or small, to write this book. It's taken a long time to bring it to fruition.

The sons of two of my father's prison camp roommates have been invaluable: John Carson in Australia and Colin Cordwell in the USA. John, having read my first few chapters, gave me the encouragement I needed to continue. Without his father's account of the Long March, which John happily shared with me, I would never have known what my own father endured.

Colin provided some great stories of our dad's shared experiences. Maybe I'll visit his pub in Chicago one day to see his collection of WW2 memorabilia, who knows?

Thanks also go to Kelvin Youngs, who runs the amazing http:// aircrewremembered.com website and was able to put me in touch with Colin.

Ben van Drogenbroek & Steve Martin, expert historians who run the Facebook group 'Stalag Luft 3 – the Great Escape – Prisoners of War,' provided me with a wealth of information, as did many of their contributors.

Jason Warr, who owns a collection of RAF and SL3 artefacts that would grace a museum, kindly provided me with copies of documents directly relating to my father's captivity.

Thanks also to Christopher Dean of the RAF Waddington Heritage Centre, who provided so much helpful information about the Augsburg Raid.

Finally, special thanks go to Cathy, my wife, whose patience, encouragement, and support have enabled me to complete my long journey through writing this book.

Author Bio

John Garwell, the eldest of Arthur and Joan Garwell's two sons, was born in London in 1948 and grew up in Epping, Essex.

He had no intention of becoming an author until, after retiring from work, he decided to read the bundle of letters that his father had sent from a German POW camp during World War II and realised that he had an extraordinary story to tell.

He now lives in the Yorkshire Dales with Cathy, his wife of 27 years, Nancy, their ageing Cockapoo, and five bicycles.

Lightning Source UK Ltd.
Milton Keynes UK
UKHW021828181122
412450UK00011B/142